THE MODERN CONSERVATIVE

AND THE LIBERAL IMAGE

M. W. BRAINARD

with Sam Wells

THE MODERN CONSERVATIVE
AND THE LIBERAL IMAGE

Weaver, Henry Grady. *The Mainspring of Human Progress*, Foundation for Economic Education, Inc., 1962.
Bastiat, C.F., *The Law*, Foundation for Economic Education, Inc., 1998.
Hazlitt, Henry, *Economics In One Lesson*, Foundation for Economic Education, Inc., 2014.
Harper, F. A. *Why Wages Rise*, Foundation for Economic Education, Inc., 1957.
Hayek, F.A., *The Road to Serfdom*, Univ. of Chicago Press, 2007.

iUniverse books may be ordered through booksellers or by contacting:

iUniverse
1663 Liberty Drive
Bloomington, IN 47403
www.iuniverse.com
1-800-Authors (1-800-288-4677)

ISBN: 978-1-5320-1983-8 (sc)
ISBN: 978-1-5320-1984-5 (e)

Print information available on the last page.

iUniverse rev. date: 03/22/2017

This study of THE MODERN CONSERVATIVE and his solid foundation is based on five outstanding books––each of which builds from the most basic fundamentals.

These books are:

1. THE MAINSPRING OF HUMAN PROGRESS
   by Henry Grady Weaver

2. WHY WAGES RISE
   by Dr. F. A. Harper

3. ECONOMICS IN ONE LESSON
   by Henry Hazlitt

4. THE ROAD TO SERFDOM
   by Friedrich A. Hayek

5. THE LAW
   by Frederic Bastiat

The special condensations of these books constitute Chapters III to VII. All works published by the Foundation for Economic Education, Irvington-On-Hudson, New York, are covered by FEE's general grant of permission to reprint, in whole or in part.

THE COVER PICTURE

correctly portrays

THE MODERN CONSERVATIVE

as an alert citizen, peaceful and intelligent, standing firmly on the solid foundation of TRUTH, KNOWLEDGE, JUSTICE and MORALITY. This is the exact opposite of the image projected by the extreme liberals who try to picture the conservative as greedy, bigoted and self-centered, shrouded in a fog of fear and mired in a swamp of hate.

Table of Contents

Illustrations and Charts

CHAPTER

1

WHAT IS A CONSERVATIVE?

The Classical or European Conservative started as a rather stodgy and bigoted feudal individual who favored a strong but "just" government. He believed in "the divine right of kings," the propriety of Lords to rule serfs and of the clergy to set moral standards and compel obedience thereto.

The Classical Liberal, as the opposite of the Conservative, opposed all forms of what we now call Big Government. He believed in maximum individual liberty as warranted by acceptance of corresponding personal responsibility and that "the least government was the best government." In this country he often is described as a Jeffersonian Liberal.

Nearly a century ago the Marxists and later, but much more effectively, the Fabian Socialists began a studied campaign to promote socialism by gradually changing the meaning of words so that words with a "good" connotation would apply to them and their activities and "bad" words to anti-socialists.

The favorable term Liberal was one of their first captives and now, to most people, it means a proponent of the welfare state. The modern Liberal still claims close association with Freedom, but it is a freedom *from* instead of freedom *to* which is the only one which corresponds to individual liberty.

The unfavorable term Conservative had to maintain its natural opposition to Liberal and thus, almost by default, it now is applied to anyone who opposes socialism in any of its many forms. Some diehard opponents of socialism refuse to accept the semantic reversal and still insist on calling themselves Liberal but most of them admit the necessity of adding the adjective Classical or Jeffersonian. Others refuse to accept the term Conservative, with its associated opprobrium, and try to find a more appropriate term such as Constitutional or Constructive. The term Constructive has a much finer connotation and certainly it is far more accurate, and thus possibly in a generation or so it may attain common usage. However, at this time the term Conservative is so widely accepted that it must be used to avoid added confusion. To be doubly sure we shall hereafter use "quotes" for both modern "Liberal" and modern "Conservative" since present usage has lost all resemblance to the basic word meanings.

The "Liberal" mantle now covers the complete range from those who advocate violent revolution (a lá the Red Chinese) to strong anti-communists who favor only mild increase in government aid to certain specific classes or causes. "Conservative" consequently must include the complete range of the opponents and thus it also has a "lunatic fringe" of "extremists" who advocate violence. However, there is considerable evidence that at least some of the wildest of these are frauds whose real purpose is to discredit the broad "conservative" movement. While each group has its noisy extremist fringe the overwhelming majority in each case is composed of people who sincerely desire peace and prosperity for all and earnestly believe that they are following the best available path thereto.

Modern "Conservatives" differ widely in both philosophy and tactics depending upon what basic aspect aroused their greatest interest and stimulated the search for further knowledge and understanding. The usual method of classification is to identify the "Conservative" by his 'anti' group as: anti-communist, anti-socialist, anti-inflationist, etc., but a more fundamental division is whether his position is based primarily on morality or economics. Both morality and economics have tremendous depth and each subject requires clear logical analysis based on fundamental truths. A casual look at either is almost certain

2

to give a wrong picture and even a fairly deep study can overlook some plausible fallacies.

During the last century science has expanded by leaps and bounds so that now many students in High School have a better understanding of basic physical laws than had the top scientists of only a generation or so ago. Modern science is rapidly unraveling the deepest secrets of the atom and the universe, and technology is applying this new knowledge to the production of new and improved products. This tremendous increase in physical engineering has so completely unbalanced its previous relationship to social engineering that now many philosophers fear that we have created a deadly Frankenstein––with present knowledge and productive capacity it would be possible to kill every person on earth and some warped minds might try to do so.

For the previous few thousand years of recorded history there was a positive balance in favor of social engineering, although admittedly the known laws were never fully obeyed. The Golden Rule and The Ten Commandments have been known for thousands of years and have their counterpart in all major religions so there would seem to be no excuse for any lack of understanding––except for one fatal factor. This factor is the inherent time-delay between cause and effect in most social actions. Strictly physical actions generally have an almost immediate final reaction but social actions, such as changes in basic moral or economic practices, may require years or even generations to fully develop the final reaction. Worse still, there usually is a temporary immediate result which is very different from the final result. This delay and ultimate reversal was aptly described by Frederic Bastiat over 100 years ago in his essay *"That Which Is Seen, and That Which Is Not Seen."*[1] The first three paragraphs follow:

"In the department of economy, an act, a habit, an institution, a law, gives birth not only to an effect, but to a series of effects. Of these effects, the first only is immediate; it manifests itself simultaneously with its cause––*it is seen*. The others unfold in succession––*they are not seen*: it is well for us, if they are *foreseen*. Between a good and a bad economist this constitutes the whole difference––the latter takes

---

[1]   The complete essay was published in 1962 by Freedom Newspapers, Inc.

account only of the visible effect; the other takes account both of the effects which are *seen*, and also of those which it is necessary to *foresee*. Now this difference is enormous, for it almost always happens that when the immediate consequence is favorable, the ultimate consequences are fatal, *and the converse*. Hence, it follows that the bad economist pursues a small present good, which will be followed by a great evil to come while the true economist pursues a great good to come at the risk of a small present evil.

"In fact, it is the same in the science of health, arts, and in that ofmorals. It often happens, that the sweeter the first fruit of a habit is, the more bitter are the consequences. Take, for example, debauchery, idleness, prodigality. When, therefore, a man absorbed in the effect which is seen, has not yet learned to discern those which are not seen, he gives way to fatal habits, not only by inclination but by calculation.

"This explains the fatally grievous condition of mankind. Ignorance surrounds its cradle: then its actions are determined by their first consequences, the only ones which, in its first stage, it can see. It is only in the long run that it learns to take account of the others. It has to learn this lesson from two very different masters––experience and foresight. Experience teaches effectually, but brutally. It makes us acquainted with all the effects of an action, by causing us to feel them; and we cannot fail to finish by knowing that fire burns, if we have burned ourselves. For this rough teacher, I should like, if possible, to substitute a more gentle one. I mean Foresight. For this purpose I shall examine the consequences of certain economical phenomena, by placing in opposition to each other those *which are seen*, and those *which are not seen*."

Bastiat then discusses a dozen typical applications which clearly demonstrate the reversal from immediate to final effect. The key points from his Chapter III, on taxes, are:

"The advantages which officials advocate are *those which are seen*. The benefit which accrues to the providers *is still that which is seen*. This blinds all eyes.

"But the disadvantages which the taxpayers have to get rid of are *those which are not seen*. And the injury which results from it to the providers, is still that *which is not seen*, although this ought to be self-evident.

"When an official spends . . . an extra hundred sous, it implies that a taxpayer spends . . . a hundred sous less; but the expense of the official is *seen*, because the act is performed, while that of the taxpayer *is not seen*, because, alas! he is prevented from performing it."

Bastiat concludes his essay with the following:

"Thus we learn, by the numerous subjects which I have treated, that, to be ignorant of political economy is to allow ourselves to be dazzled by the immediate effect of a phenomenon; to be acquainted with it is to embrace in thought and in forethought the whole compass of effects.

"I might subject a host of other questions to the same test; but I shrink from the monotony of a constantly uniform demonstration, and I conclude by applying to political economy what Chateaubriand says of history:

'There are,' he says, 'two consequences in history; an immediate one, which is instantly recognized, and one in the distance, which is not at first perceived. These consequences often contradict each other; the former are the results of our own limited wisdom, the latter, those of that wisdom which endures. The providential event appears after the human event. God rises up behind men. Deny, if you will, the supreme counsel, disown its action; dispute about words; designate, by the term, force of circumstances, or reason, what the vulgar call Providence; but look to the end of an accomplished fact, and you will see that it has always produced the contrary of what was expected from it, if it was not established at first upon morality and justice.'––*Chateaubriands Posthumous Memoirs.*"

In more modern idiom this simply states that the ultimate result of any act will be in accordance with the idea which prompted the act *only* to the extent that the idea was based on reality––on the basic laws of the universe––on things as they are––on complete understanding, not wishful thinking.[2] The ultimate result will be a reversal of the idea to the extent that the idea was not based on reality.

---

[2] The Institute for Humane Studies in Menlo Park, California was founded to probe deeply into these fundamental relationships.

This is a profound subject well worth deep consideration. Adding delicious mushrooms to a sauce adds zest to the meal and the zest and enjoyment will not be diminished if poisonous toadstools of similar taste and appearance are accidentally substituted. However, the resulting sickness will not be eliminated or even reduced because of the firm belief that the toadstools were mushrooms.

Modern "Conservatives" have at least a faint understanding of these long range reversals and the necessity for building any social order upon a firm foundation of truth, morality and justice. *They are "Conservative" just because they do have this understanding and thus are able to see past the fallacies and half-truths upon which all socialism is based.*

DEVELOPMENT OF A "CONSERVATIVE"

At 18 if a youth is not a socialist
there is something wrong with his heart.
But if at 28 he still is a socialist
there is something wrong with his head.

The above simple statement has been paraphrased in many ways but it has a basic truth which is far too little understood. In fact, if even a fair proportion of our "thought leaders" really understood the fundamentals involved we would not be enmeshed in one crisis after another.

Any intelligent, well-meaning youth readily understands the necessity for guidance and control. He respects and obeys his parents and fully approves of the respect and cooperation which they give to the leaders and officials of the church, city and state. These in turn respect and cooperate with national leaders so it is only natural for such a youth to feel that the President of the United States is one of the very wisest and best men in the world and that when he, in his great wisdom, proposes a law and the congress, with its wide understanding, polishes the rough spots, the final result must be to the great advantage of the nation as a whole even though some few people may be penalized. Such a youth is quite willing to pay his share of the costs and accept controls necessary to the proper functioning of all laws which, naturally, are for the general welfare.

As the youth matures, has more experience, and gains a deeper understanding he learns to look past the immediate and the obvious—— to look for hidden factors and attempt to foresee the long-range effects of each proposal. He is surprised to find that the immediate and obvious beneficial results of many acts are completely reversed by hidden and long-range effects which should have been foreseen.

The maturing youth is shocked to find that some officials knowingly will propose seriously objectionable propositions, which are doctored to seem beneficial and thus appeal to the mass of voters, in order to consolidate political power.

The change in an individual's acceptance of socialism, with its inherent controls, as he gains understanding of the long range evils of socialism, is shown graphically on page 15 for the two basically opposite types of individual. The evil, selfish, power-hungry individual has a strong tendency to reject all controls and thus he is against socialism until he learns that he can use the inherent controls of socialism to his personal advantage. Lord Acton was correct that "Power tends to corrupt and absolute power corrupts absolutely" so it is obvious that increased understanding and use of power by evil people causes an increasing desire for still more power and thus KNOWLEDGEABLE EVIL PEOPLE ALWAYS FAVOR MORE SOCIALISM. It is less obvious that the acquisition of power by even highly moral "do-gooders" has a strong tendency to shift them onto the "evil" curve since first they need more power in order to do more good, then they lose perspective and finally become corrupted.[1]

The opposite type of individual is helpful and kindly and has high ideals. With no understanding of the inherent evils of socialism he is quite willing to accept the associated controls and costs as obviously necessary for the general welfare. As he learns more and more about the long range evil effects inherent in all socialistic measures he becomes less and less tolerant of socialism until finally with deep understanding he becomes an "extremist" who favors zero socialism since he knows that even a little socialism is dangerous for, like a cancer, it always tends to grow bigger. In fact, the larger it gets the faster it tends to grow.

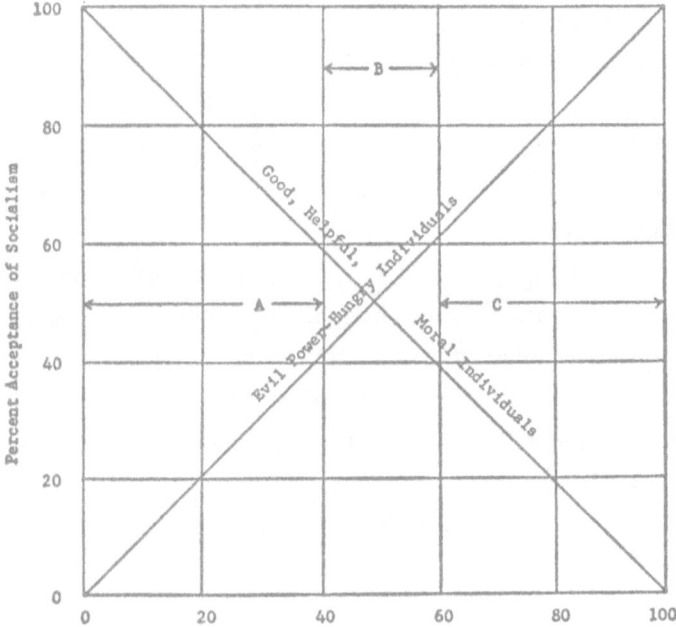

This graph shows the acceptance of socialism for any one individual, based on his personal understanding. It is divided into three sections, labeled A, B and C, and we have estimated the proportion of the adult population in each as: A- over 60%, B- about 20%, and C- under 20%. The concentration is much heavier toward the left side since most people have little knowledge of the evils inherent in socialism and only a very few have any real depth of understanding.

To better develop the full import of these facts the graph has been redrawn to indicate general voter acceptance of socialism versus general voter understanding. This is the same graph except that the people are distributed uniformly and the crossed lines then become curved to correspond.[1]

---

[1]   The assumed uniform distribution is not rigorously accurate but the fact of the great masses with little understanding more than compensates for any errors in distribution and thus the overall picture is reasonably correct.

The amazing and shocking disclosure from this revised graph is that for at least 60% of the voters (group A) the "good guys" are all in favor of considerable socialism and only the "bad guys" are against socialism. Group B, about another 20% of the voters, see no particular moral involvement since they are in the area where the curves cross. However, for those in Group C, the remaining 20% or less, who have from moderate to deep understanding, there is a definite distinction with only the power-hungry individuals favoring socialism and all moral people adamant against it.

Many politicians "go along" with popular socialistic practices, which they know to be harmful, just to help insure re-election. Thus they place themselves (as is usual with expediency) in the range between the moral an the evil. Those who accept a moderate amount of socialism (the middle-of-the-roaders) range from the moral but relatively uninformed (who believe some socialism is necessary) to the more informed but less moral who understand the inherent evils but "go along" for expediency.

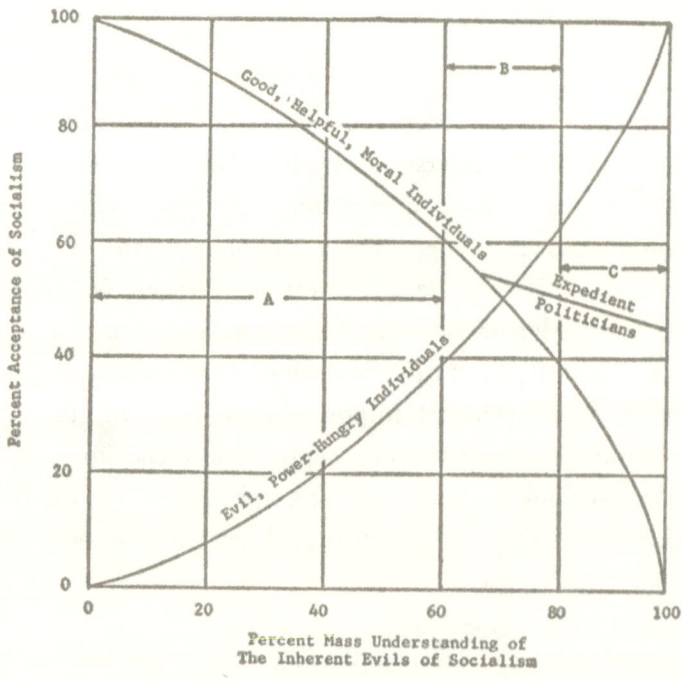

Percent Mass Understanding of
The Inherent Evils of Socialism

With over three-fourths of the people seeing nothing very "evil" about a "reasonable" degree of socialism, it is no wonder that the remaining few who do know it to be evil and thus fight it diligently are considered "extremists." Conversely, those who do know about the inherent evils of socialism simply can't understand how supposedly intelligent people can be so utterly stupid as to fall for its false utopias.

Politicians are not alone in subverting morality by expediency, for by using carefully planned cries of "extremism" the "extreme liberals" have made everything at all patriotic, constitutional, or financially stable so highly "controversial" that only a very few people have sufficient understanding or the moral courage to stand up and be counted for what they know to be right. This tendency is especially evident in business and professional men who are so fearful of offending anyone that they effectively finance and promote socialistic policies and candidates.

A good example is the merchant who places double page spreads in the local "liberal" paper but would not dare place a quarter page ad in a "conservative" paper even though he knew that dollar for dollar it would attract far more in sales.

Possibly a better example is the doctor who supplies his waiting room with "liberal" magazines which in stories as well as feature articles and editorials advocate all forms of socialism (including Medicare). He knows that the proposals are demoralizing and generally uneconomic and that Medicare is a definite threat to his patient's health and well-being, as well as to his own business, but he is so afraid of being "controversial" that he does nothing about it.

Constructive Action was formed in 1963 for the specific purpose of supplying doctors, and others, with a full range of constructive books, pamphlets, magazines, newspapers and newsletters suitable for the waiting room or lobby. The cost was negligible (about the equivalent of two to five minutes per day) and the effect could have been tremendous, especially if each doctor had made special mention of some pertinent item to each patient. With this service in most of the waiting rooms the "liberal" blockade of news would have been sufficiently pierced to allow considerable exposure of the half-truths of socialism to reach the general public. The "liberal" induced fear of "controversy" stopped the program cold for after spending tens of thousands of dollars and untold hours developing the program, preparing the material and promoting its use, the subscribers reached a maximum of only one doctor out of a few thousand instead of the expected high percentage.

"Conservatives" basically are individualists and as they wish to avoid controversy they are easily duped into the actual promotion and financing of socialistic policies and projects. They delude themselves with the idea that they must be "practical"; that they are in business to make a profit and that ideology is strictly political and must not be mixed with business. They forget that while immediate profit is desirable, it must never be allowed to ruin the business itself and that *the surest way to ruin all business is to allow socialism to strangle our free economy.*

For all who doubt this or consider it as "extreme conservatism" it is suggested that they reserve judgment until they have read this book in its entirety and given careful consideration to the facts as presented by the various authors. What now seems just "good business" may then seem more the betrayal of our entire civilization for a "few pieces of silver."

Giving to "liberal" churches is another way in which "conservatives" (who supply much of the money) contribute directly and vitally to the advancement of socialism.

It has been aptly stated that "WHEN FREEDOM IS AT STAKE, SILENCE IS NOT GOLDEN––IT IS JUST PLAIN YELLOW."

A main theme of Bill Richardson's little book, *Slightly To The Right*, is how the public has been conditioned to reject "conservative" arguments and what is needed to overcome such rejection. However, even full knowledge of such conditioning does not greatly reduce the shock to a knowledgeable "conservative" when his friends and associates pay no attention to his warnings of serious danger ahead.

He knows that these people do care deeply about what happens to their children and grandchildren and that they would gladly devote their lives to the preservation and improvement of civilization so, obviously, the lack of attention to his warnings is not simple apathy. He knows also that they are not too stupid to understand the clear logic of his arguments and since normally they are quite willing to discuss and argue he is forced to the most unpleasant conclusion that they refuse to even listen to his arguments because they consider him "cracked" on the subject.

Such rejection causes many really good thinkers to "clam-up" just when they should be working most diligently and this book is intended to give them the information and inspiration to keep up the fight. In many cases the danger of receiving such unintended insult can be avoided by making your appeal practically irresistible. When presenting a controversial book or idea, tell your friend that you do not expect him to agree with all points expressed but that you do desire to have a discussion-in-depth on the subject at his earliest convenience. A dinner engagement or other specific date for discussion usually insures prompt and careful attention.

Since the modern "conservative" is a conservative just because he does have some depth of understanding regarding the long-range evils inherent in socialism, any analysis of his position should start from the basis of his understanding. The really knowledgeable "conservative" has a wide base of deep understanding of fundamental moral and economic principles and the history of their application and violation. Most "conservatives," however, understand only limited aspects or certain particular applications and have only a vague knowledge of the basic principles.

The three main foundations for truly constructive thinking are:

1. Moral——the most basic foundation.
2. Economic——fundamental economic laws are based on morality.
3. Historical——knowledge that improved human well-being invariably follows individual freedom and that freedom can exist only in a moral society with individual responsibility.

To give a firm foundation we shall outline the basic principles and give a detailed review, by quote and comment, of five carefully selected books. Each book so reviewed is recognized as basic in its field and further references are given for more advanced study in specific subjects. Some of the quotes are condensed; i.e., a paragraph may be composed of sentences taken from two or three paragraphs, but in each such case care has been taken to prevent distortion of the original meaning.

We start with a short review of the rise and fall of human wellbeing and its relation to the acceptance or violation of basic economic and moral principles. The primary book for this study is the little gem, *Mainspring Of Human Progress* by Henry Grady Weaver.

CHAPTER III

THE MAINSPRING OF HUMAN PROGRESS

"Why did men die of starvation for 6,000 years? Why is it that we in America have never had a famine?"

Mainspring is much more than a history of human prosperity for it also asks *why* each civilization prospered and then declined and it outlines why Western civilization is now at such a high level. It discusses the forces and principles which produced this prosperity and also some which are antagonistic.

Written in 1947 by Henry Grady Weaver, who specialized in the dramatization of difficult data, as head of Customer Research for General Motors Corporation, *Mainspring* is an outstanding example of his ability. It has run through many printings and its wide acceptance warranted a 1965 reprint with a new cover, plus an excellent bibliography, at a reduced price.

Mainspring is so clear and concise that one is embarrassed to attempt a condensation and it must be emphasized that much of interest and value *has* been left out while selecting only the key elements which were especially pertinent to this study.

PART I   COMPARISONS AND CONTRASTS

Puzzling Questions

"Why did families live for 6,000 years in caves and floorless hovels, without windows or chimneys––then within a few generations, we in America take floors, rugs, chairs, tables, windows, and chimneys for granted and regard electric lights, refrigerators, running water, porcelain baths, and toilets as common necessities?

"Why did men, women, and children eke out their meager existence for 6,000 years, toiling desperately from dawn to dark––barefoot, half-naked, unwashed, unshaved, uncombed, with lousy hair, mangy skins, and rotting teeth––then suddenly, in one place on earth there is an abundance. . . . ?"

Weaver then shows that other places and peoples have as good natural resources and individual skill and intelligence but that somehow "we, in the United States of America, have made more effective use of our human energies than have any other people on the face of the globe––anywhere or at any time." If this is true, and it seems obvious, the problem reduces to "why does human energy work better here than anywhere else? And answering that question leads us into a whole string of questions, such as:

1.   What is the nature of human energy?
2.   How does it differ from other forms of energy?
3.   What makes it work?
4.   What are the things that keep it from working?
5.   How can it be made to work better? more efficiently? more effectively?

"In the last analysis, poverty, famine, and the devastations of war are all traceable to a lack of understanding of human energy and to a failure to use it to the best advantage.

"History affords abundant evidence in support of that statement; but the evidence is somewhat obscured because most of the textbooks stress war and conflict, rather than the causes of war and what might be done to prevent war."

Weaver then discusses human energy and shows that it, "like any other energy, operates according to certain natural laws. For one thing, it works only under its own natural control." One of the laws is that each individual controls his own thoughts and actions and he concludes that there are two main points involved:

"1. Individual freedom is the natural heritage of each living person.
2. Freedom cannot be separated from responsibility."

He also emphasizes that "man is different because he is a human being; and as a human being, he has the power of reason, the power of imagination, the ability to capitalize on the experiences of the past and present as bearing on the problems of the future. He has the ability to change *himself* as well as his environment. He has the ability to progress and to keep on progressing."

The Great Multiplier

"Through foresight, imagination, and individual initiative, man develops tools and facilities which expand his efforts and enable him to produce things which would not otherwise be possible. This is an outstanding difference between man and animal, just as it is an outstanding difference between civilization and barbarism."

A short discussion of the necessity for tools concludes that "the main point is that the introduction of tools marked the beginning of man's progress in three important directions:

1. More effective use of energy.
2. Specialization of effort.
3. Advances in human cooperation and improvements in living conditions, through the peaceful exchange of goods and services.

Also, the introduction of tools brought into sharper focus the importance of individual property rights. Unless a person has a chance of gaining some direct benefit from his extra efforts, there is not much inducement for him to think ahead and to make the sacrifices necessary to provide the tools of production. And without the tools of production, human beings would sink back into a state of barbarism."

Networks and Pitfalls

"The modern world is an intricate network of living human energies linking all persons in co-operative effort and in one common fate.

"Do unto others as you would have them do unto you is not only a sound moral precept, it is also the hardheaded advice of practical self-interest. Whoever injures another injures himself because he decreases the opportunities for gain that come through co-operation and exchange.

"But how can we reconcile the principle of co-operation with the conflicts of competition? The answer is that there is nothing inconsistent between the two. Competition is the practical manifestation of human beings in free control of their individual affairs arriving at a balance in their relationships with one another. Free competition is, within itself, a co-operative process."

Weaver discusses some problems of co-operation and competition and shows how easy it is to become convinced that some centralized control of human energies could "run things the way they ought to be run."

"At one time or another, every conceivable form of authority has been tried, but each has failed for the simple reason that:

1. Only an individual human being can generate human energy.
2. Only an individual human being can control the energy he generates.

The lack of understanding of these simple, basic truths has, for over 6,000 years, stagnated human progress and kept the vast majority of people underfed, poorly clothed, embroiled in wars, and dying from famine and pestilence."

He concludes that "Individuals direct their energies and build their organizations according to their views of reality––what they conceive to be desirable and good.

"Since the actions of any individual are determined by his beliefs, it follows that the underlying control of the energies of any group of persons is the religious faith prevailing among them." These may be classified as: Pagan, non-pagan, or some combination of the two.

PART II   THE OLD WORLD VIEW

"The pagan has a fatalistic outlook on life. He believes that the individual is helpless; that he is wholly at the mercy of relentless forces outside of himself; that there's nothing he can do to improve his lot.

"From the pagan viewpoint, man is not self-controlling, not responsible for his own acts. The pagan universe is timeless, changeless, static. There is no such thing as progress. Most human beings cling to the ancient superstitions that they are not self-controlling and not responsible for their own acts.

"One of the oldest, if not *the* oldest, form of pagan worship is based on the idea that human destiny is controlled by the over-all will-of-the-tribe, rather than by the initiative and free will of the individual persons who make up the tribe.

"The welfare of this mystic being is called 'the common good,' which is supposed to be more important than the good of the individual. It was precisely in that spirit that the ancient Aztec priest thrust a knife into the human victim on the altar and, with holy incantations, tore out the bleeding heart. The real human world is made by persons, not by societies. The only human development is the self-development of the individual person. There is no short cut!

"But even today, many civilized persons––nice people, cultured, gentle, and kind, our friends and our neighbors, almost all of us at some time or another––have harbored the pagan belief that the sacrifice of the individual person serves a higher good. The superstition lingers in the false ideal of selflessness––which emphasizes conformity to the will-of-the-mass––as against the Christian virtues of self-reliance, self-improvement, self-faith, self-respect, self-discipline, and a recognition of one's *duties* as well as one's *rights*.

"Such thinking is promoted under the banner of social reform, but it gives rise to the tyrants of 'do-goodism'––the führers, the dictators, the overlords. The harm done by ordinary criminals, murderers, gangsters, and thieves is negligible in comparison with the agony inflicted upon human beings by the professional 'do-gooders' who attempt to set themselves up as gods on earth and who would ruthlessly force their views on all others––with the abiding assurance that the end justifies the means.

"But it is a mistake to assume that the do-gooders are insincere. The danger lies in the fact that their faith is just as devout and just as ardent as that of the ancient Aztec priest."

Socialism and/or Communism

Weaver takes a page to review socialism and communism and show how Marx completely misinterpreted the trend toward industrialization while Bastiat foretold accurately how increased tooling and increased production would mean increased prosperity for all classes.

All forms of collectivism are based on the pagan belief that the "common good" is more important than the individual and that "progress" demands central planning. Then, "Human energy and individual initiative are put in a straight jacket, and the inevitable result is poverty and distress leading into war. It may be internal rebellion, or it may be a war of aggression against other people. Those in power naturally prefer the latter course. It provides the opportunity to draw attention away from failures at home, with the alluring possibility of taking wealth from others––and getting away with it.

"In all fairness, it must be said that communism recognizes human equality and the brotherhood of man––in theory at least. But it fails to recognize the *real nature* of man. The communist has not yet seen the fallacy in the ancient, infantile assumption that individual persons are controlled by some superindividual authority. He does not question this pagan superstition. He takes it for granted.

"Other collectivist societies are not quite so organized. But the misguided benevolence of complete social and economic power always leads to ruthless suppression of religious freedom, personal freedom, freedom of expression, and even freedom of thought."

The Living Authorities

Weaver discusses various types of monarchs and shows that: "Whether the monarch is looked upon as a living god or as God's personal agent, all property is at his disposal; and in practice, he bestows great wealth and the exercise of some authority on a few persons, who then form a superior class––nobles, samurai, aristocrats, bureaucratic ministers in control of this, that, and the other. Such men, headed by their emperor, their king, or their queen, are looked upon as the government."

One of the surprising advantages of a living monarch over ancient communism is the break in control when changing rulers and that: "The superficialities of court life provide an outlet for royal energy that is less harmful, and far less expensive, than unintelligent meddling.

"In any few hundred years of Old World history, we find a succession of convulsive efforts and collapses––as if a living thing were roped down and struggling.

"That is precisely what was happening. Human energy could not get to work at its primary, natural job of producing and distributing the necessities of human life. Whenever men began to develop farming and crafts and trade, government stopped them.

"Mind you, the government never intended to stop them; indeed, its honest aim was to help them. But the effect was the opposite, for the simple reason that efforts to help were based on the false notion that human energy and individual initiative can be directed and controlled through an overriding authority, using the brute force of military and police power." Force can be used properly only for protection and any other use cannot lead to best mental and moral growth.

"Human energy cannot operate effectively except when men are free to act and to be responsible for their actions. But liberty does not mean license; for no one has a right to infringe upon the rights of others. Certain restraints are necessary, and they are provided in two ways:

1. *Legal restraints*—the passing of laws to be administered by governmental agencies and enforced by police power.
2. *Moral restraints*—which depend upon individual self-discipline, logical reasoning, good sportsmanship, and a consideration for the rights of others.

"It's easy to say 'Let's settle this or that by passing a law.' But laws on the statue books can never be an adequate substitute for moral restraint based on enlightened self-interest—which means a recognition of one's duties as well as one's rights.

"The extension of laws into areas where they cannot be enforced does more harm than good:

1. It takes emphasis away from personal responsibility and promotes the dangerous notion that legalized force can be used as a substitute for self-control and individual morality.
2. It increases red tape and government overhead, without accomplishing the intended result.
3. It weakens respect for the really necessary laws.
4. Law observance breaks down and remedy is sought in bolstering the penalties and in passing additional laws.
5. Along with it all, the administrative and enforcement facilities are further increased, which means taking more and more people away from productive work.

"Any attempt to give to government the responsibilities which properly belong to the individual citizens works at cross-purposes to the advancement of personal freedom. It retards progress—morally as well as along the lines of greater productivity.

"Progress lies in working in harmony with the fundamental nature of man, not in reverting to the pagan superstition which, for over 6,000 years, has suppressed individual initiative and kept human energy in a strait jacket.

"In modern times, this pagan superstition is known by the persuasive name *planned economy*, which is nothing more than a weasel word for socialism or communism or fascism.

"It is difficult for Americans to understand the stagnating effects of regimentation and how it leads to greater and greater oppressions. It is generally outside the range of our experience because we have lived in a new kind of world where human energy and initiative have usually worked under the natural control of the individual––which is the only way that they can ever work effectively."

The Static Center

"There is no denying the fact that human beings progress and prosper in proportion to the degree to which individual initiative is permitted, or at least *not* prevented.

"This explains the historical fact––at first surprising––that a sincere, conscientious, hard-working ruler always does the most harm to his own subjects. The lazy, dissolute ruler neglects his job. Caligula, for instance, merely wasted goods in riotous extravagance and tortured just a few hundred of his subjects for his personal enjoyment. The majority of the people always get along comparatively well under a ruler like Caligula.

"It was the sober, ascetic, industrious Augustus Caesar, toiling for the welfare of his Empire and its people, who began the destruction of Rome and laid the foundation for the misery and human degradation which Europeans suffered for centuries thereafter. He launched a planned economy which was to serve as the basis for the Roman world peace.

"The hairsplitting economic regulations were perfected by Diocletian, whose stern directives were so efficiently administered that farmers could no longer farm; . . . There was no work for the working man, so the beneficial government stepped in and, by taxing the rich, managed for awhile to provide the populace with bread and circus tickets.

"But that was no solution. The improvement was short-lived. Money can't buy goods unless the goods are produced.

"The mounting taxes put more and more people out of business. An increasing number of workers were forced onto tax-supported relief until there was not enough productive energy at work to pay the tax bills. The great Roman Empire––with its plans for a thousand years of peace and security––collapsed into the Dark Ages.

"That was the work of the *best* of emperors."

Weaver then discusses England, France and Germany, and shows that the tremendous growth of the British Empire came under very weak monarchs while France and Germany were under such strict governments that great expansion was impossible. He tells of perpetual famines and how some people still live as their ancestors have lived for thousands of years, regardless of all the fine plans of the rulers to improve society. He continues: "If men and women do not want to live like that––if they do not want to be always in destitution, always on the verge of starvation––they must come to realize that they, and they alone, can control their human energies. No possible use of physical force can compel anyone to think, speak, or act. It can only limit, hinder, and prevent.

"In the last analysis, and stripped of all the furbelows, government is nothing more than a legal monopoly of the use of physical force––by persons upon persons."

Weaver discusses the innumerable revolts against some particular authority, or type of authority, "without disturbing the pagan belief that *some* authority should control their lives and be responsible for their welfare." These revolts were not true revolutions as they were just a change of authority––king to despot to bureaucracy to dictator to king, etc. "There have been 6,000 years of it; and for 6,000 years people have gone hungry. The simple reason is that human energy cannot be made to work efficiently except in an atmosphere of individual freedom and voluntary co-operation, based on enlightened self-interest and moral responsibility.

"There has never been but one real revolution. It is the revolution against pagan fatalism––the revolution for *human freedom*."

PART III   THE REVOLUTION

The First Attempt

Weaver traces the first recorded attempt of a true revolution against pagan superstition back in biblical history in the era of Abraham and Moses. "Abraham denied the existence of all these pagan gods. He taught his increasing family that God is Rightness, Reality, and Truth; that man is free and self-controlling and responsible for his own acts; that each person is free to do good or evil, as he may choose, but that any wrong act will result in punishment to the evildoer.

"So long as men labored under the delusion that the universe is controlled by the whims and fancies of prankish gods, there was no point in trying to improve anything through individual effort. Progress did not come until men began to realize that everything works according to a divine plan, the essence of which is truth and rightness. This applies not only to questions of morality, but also to all other things. Every engineer, every scientist, every farmer, and every mechanic knows that nothing will work, and no act will succeed, unless it is in harmony with rightness—the true nature of things as they are."

The story continues through Joseph and his special planned economy which reduced the Egyptian farmers to virtual serfs—the Egyptian revolt which turned the tables, and the final rescue of the Israelites by Moses followed by forty years of wandering in the desert. "They wanted Moses to be their king so that they could hold him responsible and blame him for everything. But Moses turned them down and kept on insisting that they were free, responsible for themselves, that there was no pagan god to control them and be responsible for them; that no man could rule another man. But the children of Israel kept on murmuring, drifting back into idolatry, and sneaking every chance to worship their pagan gods."

THE TEN COMMANDMENTS

"Finally, as a last resort, Moses reduced the teachings of Abraham to a written code of moral law. Known as the 'Ten Commandments,' it stands today as the first and greatest document of individual freedom in the recorded history of man. Each of the Ten Commandments is addressed to the individual as a self-controlling person responsible for his own thoughts, words, and acts. And each of them recognizes liberty and freedom as inherent in the nature of man.

"The first commandment tells the individual to reject pagan gods and recognize his own worth as a human being, subject to no power but that of the Creator and Judge.

"The second tells the individual to form no image of abstract rightness, but to direct his reverence toward the divine in truth.

"The third tells the individual not to speak frivolously of the Creator and Judge. Knowledge of fundamental truth——cause and effect——is of first importance and should be taken very seriously.

"The fourth tells the individual to devote some time (one day out of seven) to reflection on the eternal verities.

"The fifth recognizes the family as the primary human relationship and establishes the parent's authority over the child as the only authority which the child should accept for his own profit.

"The sixth stresses the sanctity of human life——the individual's right to live, which is a right that must not be violated by any other person.

"The seventh establishes the principle of contract——the inviolability of promises given by persons to each other and the double sanctity of the marriage contract, which is the basis of the family.

"The eighth recognizes the individual's right to his own property.

"The ninth recognizes free speech——the individual's control over his own utterances and his responsibility for their truth.

"The tenth emphasizes again the right of ownership. Not even in thought should a person violate the property rights of another."

It should be emphasized that every one of these basic precepts is a necessary prerequisite to a full flowering of human happiness and prosperity. It is impossible to conceive of such a society where:

(1, 2, & 3) The people were basically controlled by human lusts and drives for power and luxury instead of striving for self-improvement and self-responsibility.

(4 & 5) The people did not make a regular and consistent effort to improve their understanding of the eternal truths; and children did not bother to learn from their parents.

(6) Human life was not respected and one must spend his best efforts toward killing his enemies and to prevent them from killing him.

(7) There were no family ties to encourage saving and increased productivity.

(8 & 10) Any property in excess of that required for immediate consumption would be stolen unless great care was taken for its protection.

(9) Promises and contracts were unreliable. Our entire prosperity is based on the division of labor and this in turn on honored agreements––the practical certainity that agreements will be fulfilled.

"The Decalogue of Moses is one of the most amazing statements of truth ever written, but it was too revolutionary to find acceptance in the pagan world of his time; the ancient Israelites wanted a king rather than a code of personal conduct."

For generations the Israelites begged to have a king to rule over them and finally they had their way but the ideas of right and freedom did not entirely perish.

THE NEW COMMANDMENT

"Christ came upon the earth 2,000 years after the time of Abraham. He spoke of the God of Abraham, the God of Truth, the God of Rightness––the God who does not control any man, but who judges the acts of every man.

"Christ illustrated His teachings with practical examples––simple parables and stories expressed in terms of personal relations between individuals. Most important of all, He brought a new commandment which is the foundation of intelligent self-interest and practical co-operation: 'Love thy neighbor as thyself.' 'Whatsoever ye would that men should do to you, do ye even so to them.' 'Inasmuch as ye have done *it* unto one of the least of these my brethren, ye have done *it* unto me.'

"Although gentle and kindly, Christ was a fighter who brought a sword of truth to destroy the pagan kingdoms. He rendered unto Caesar the things that were Caesar's, but only the things that force could take––a coin, a material thing, even life itself––never freedom. In sermons and parables and acts Christ always asserted individual freedom. 'The kingdom of God is within you.'"

Compromise

"Abraham declared that every man is a free agent, responsible only to God. Moses reduced the teachings of Abraham to a written code of moral law, directed to the individual. Christ expanded on these teachings and added a new commandment emphasizing the principle of human brotherhood.

"These events marked the turning point in a world which had long been dominated by the gods of superstition––the will-of-the-swarm and the living authorities.

"The new teachings were too revolutionary to be accepted all at once; even down to this day, they have never been given a thorough trial. But their impact on the deep-seated superstitions was terrific; and history since the time of Christ is largely a record of conflicts and compromises between paganism and freedom."

Weaver continues with an interesting account of the beginnings of freedom in Greece and Rome until "The advance of Christianity in Europe resulted in the rise of the feudal system. In a sense, the feudal system resembled communism, except that it was set up on a stratified basis.

"The absence of responsibility and the freedom from the urge of ambition were not without their compensations. Discontent was reduced, and each class had some degree of economic security.

"But the specialization of effort and the systemization of war made it possible for human energy to work with some degree of effectiveness. Famines became less frequent. Some of the peasants grew so prosperous that they even wore shoes on holidays, when merry crowds thronged to watch men and women burned alive at the stake, broken on the wheel, or hanged, drawn, and quartered.

"Even in Catholic countries, Europeans began to accept the theory that the king partakes of the divinity of God and that the child of a king is the natural heir to this divine endowment. This compromise was a backward step. In Europe, it wrecked the feudal system, the existence of which depended on maintaining a communal balance between classes. The reversion to pagan beliefs upset this balance and resulted in nationalism and war.

"Only in Britain was the feudal system kept intact—properly balanced and improved. On their sea-guarded island, the British barons successfully resisted their kings. At Runnymede in the year 1215, their armed forces so frightened King John that he signed an agreement to respect feudal customs.

"The Magna Carta was an admission from the King that his power was not unlimited. As a written statement of British liberties, it has preserved the best values of the feudal system and has served as the foundation for building the British Empire.

"But a grant of freedom is a denial of the fact that the individual is naturally free. A thing that can be given to one person by another person can also be taken away."

The Second Attempt

This chapter is a most interesting account of the rise and fall of the Saracen civilization which is largely unknown to all but a few true scholars. Their marvelous improvements on previous cultures filtered back to Europe at the time of the Crusades and furnished the basis for ending the Dark Ages.

Prelude to the Third Attempt

Weaver outlines the discoveries of Columbus, Balboa, De Soto, etc., the mass deportation of the Moors from Spain and the building of the great Spanish Empire.

"But there was a weakness at the core. Not only had the energetic Moriscos been exterminated, but also for three generations the most self-reliant of Spain's young men had been leaving their native land to seek fame and fortune in the New World. Others had gone to the European wars.

"The people at home had been won over to the alluring theory of authoritarian control. They were losing their self-reliance with their independence. As in the case of Greece and Rome, it was the beginning of the end. In three generations––from grandfather to grandson––the concept of individual freedom was all but forgotten.

"In the meantime, while Spain was busy strengthening its central government and extending its planned economy, England was drifting in the opposite direction.

"Under the reign of Queen Elizabeth, the British government became so badly disorganized and so weak that the people were thrown on their own resources. It was 'root hog or die' and private citizens rose to the occasion––with telling effects.

"Unwittingly, without conscious intent and with no centralized planning, the foundation was being laid for a new empire based on trade and commerce. In the eyes of the European powers, England had degenerated into near-anarchy. But when the 'invincible' Spanish Armada sailed forth to capture the island, Francis Drake and his hastily assembled fleet of motley privateers defeated them soundly.

"It was a turning point in world history, and Spain never quite recovered.

"The days of the conquistadors were over. The Spanish colonies were beginning to stagnate under bureaucratic controls administered from faraway Madrid. The stream of riches which had been pouring in from the New World was slowing down. Domestic industry had almost ceased to exist. Government overhead was completely out-of-bounds.

"Things went from bad to worse, and after two more generations, the people of Spain were not getting enough food to keep alive. Unpaid soldiers left the frontiers unguarded and ravaged the countryside. Vast areas of fertile land were abandoned, the rural population flocked to the cities in search of food, just as a fisherman might seek dry land in a frantic effort to change his luck. When people get into the habit of depending on some centralized authority to provide the things which they alone can produce, mob psychology always takes hold, and they flock to the cities.

"The government could no longer get even a dribble of taxes from provinces which had formerly filled the royal treasury to overflowing. Tax collectors tore down private homes and sold the materials to raise money. In some towns they demolished more than half the dwellings.

"The day of reckoning was at hand. For too long, the people had been lulled into false complacency. For too long, they had been taught to expect some centralized authority to run their lives and provide for their needs. Human energy had ceased to function. Spain, as a great power, had ceased to exist.

"But across the sea, a new civilization was in the making––a civilization more closely resembling that of the Saracens than anything which had gone before.

The Third Attempt

"Abraham and the prophets knew that men are free. Christ knew it. The Saracens knew it. And 200 years after the fall of Granada, the idea was gaining momentum along the eastern edge of North America.

"Obscure individuals––who lived and died unknown to anyone but their neighbors––started the third attempt to establish conditions in which human beings could use their natural freedom.

"This third revolutionary effort has hardly begun. There are men living today whose grandfathers helped to begin it. Yet it was started when gods in human form were believed to govern most of the earth's population; where kings by divine right owned Continental Europe and most of the New World."

Weaver discusses the careful planning for the French and Spanish colonies and the almost complete lack thereof along New England. "In the eyes of the carefully selected and well-regimented French and Spanish, the English colonists were a scandal. Their villages were unplanned. . . . There was no co-ordination. They didn't cultivate their crops communally. Their harvests were not shared equally. They had little respect for constituted authority.

"The English colonies were often split up as a result of internal dissensions and clashing views. Rebels would pull out, push farther inland, and start new settlements. All in all, they were wild and undisciplined subjects of bad rulers; and to the Spanish and the French, the word *Bostonian* came to mean a lawless, devil-may-care sort of person––quite the opposite of what it means today.

"It is no exaggeration to say that, in the main, the people sent over by the early trading companies were the rag, tag, and bobtail of Europe–– hungry wretches lucky to be out of debtors' prisons, vagrants from highways and slums. They came at their own risk and with no guarantee of security.

"Some of them were shanghaied; others sold themselves into slavery to pay for their passage. And there were shiploads of women who were auctioned off at the ports to settlers in need of wives.

"The Spanish, French, and Dutch came over in order to extend the power of their home governments; but the English more often than not, came over to escape the domination of Old World monarchs. Among them were people in search of greater religious freedom, including the Pilgrims and the Quakers, who, back in England, were looked upon as the religious fanatics of their time.

"About the only aristocrats among the early settlers were the younger sons, the poor relations, and the black sheep of the European gentry. But they were in the minority, and the American wilderness showed no favors. These were times when even a gentleman had to work––or starve. No one of the aristocratic class had ever faced such a choice. And those in the lower classes were in an even worse predicament. They had always depended on someone else to provide them with jobs. But on this side of the world, jobs didn't exist. They had to create their own jobs. They had to use their heads, as well as their hands. It was either that or starve.

"They were up against stern reality, and no one could afford the illusion that anyone other than his own will controlled his productive powers. Each came to realize that the only source of wealth is human energy attacking this earth; that he alone was responsible for his life; that if he didn't save it, nothing would.

"Thus, the slipshod practices of the early trading companies served to plant the seeds of self-reliance. From the very beginning, it was 'root hog or die'; and in the desperate effort to survive, they were learning how to wrest a pretty good living from the American wilderness."

The story continues about the Quakers and the Cavaliers; and especially the Oglethorpes of Georgia who had a marvelous plan for controlled colonization: "In spite of his self-sacrifice and high motives, Oglethorpe's venture was a miserable failure from an economic and sociological standpoint. He failed to recognize that military regimentation works at cross-purposes to creative progress––that human initiative doesn't operate according to the pattern of a beehive.

"During 20 years of futile effort, the population never exceeded 6,000; and when it dwindled back down to around 500, Oglethorpe gave up in despair and returned to England.

"A few years later, all the bans and prohibitions were lifted. Things were thrown wide open. 'Refugees' who had fled to the Carolinas came back and brought their friends with them, and there was an influx of new blood from Virginia––including the cavalier Talbots. The last of the 13 colonies grew by leaps and bounds; and by the end of the century, its population had passed the 160,000 mark.

"Oglethorpe's effort to set up a Utopia was one of the most extreme attempts at regimentation; but it is typical, in many respects, of the type of thing that laid the groundwork for the revolution that was to come."

The Roots of Revolution

Weaver outlines the growth of the American colonies under the negligent rule of Charles II and discusses the Old World philosophers' shock at the dawn of the Age of Science and their reversion to even stricter planning. In England "The first two Georges had been rather prone to take things easy. They hadn't even bothered to learn the English language and had depended largely on their ministers to run things.

"With George III, it was going to be different. He was only twenty-two when he came to the throne, but he was a hard worker and a stickler for detail. For the first time in generations, England had a conscientious ruler. In common with his cousin, Frederick the Great, young George was an ardent admirer of the European intellectuals, who were still looking for an enlightened despot to put their theories into effect.

"Time and circumstances offered big opportunities for the new king. England had been too loosely governed. The planning had been inadequate. For too long, the colonists had been flouting the authority of the Crown. Something must be done, and George III was the man to do it. Spurred on by an ambitious mother, he intended to bring to the English people the benefits of law and order––with systematic regimentation in the best Prussian manner."

The story continued with his plans and failures, all of which greatly antagonized the colonists. ". . . . at last, the British government was compelled to use the only power that any state has at its disposal––the power of brute force used with general consent. But when the King's troops were moved into Boston to take things over, the Americans did not consent. They stood their ground as free individuals, and they fought the British Regulars.

"The great fact in history is this: *The American Revolution had no leader.* This fact is the hope of the world because human freedom is a personal matter. Only the individual can protect human rights in the infinite complexity of men's relationships with each other. Nothing on earth is more valuable than the person who knows that all men are free and who accepts the responsibilities that go with freedom.

"The pioneer Americans knew that they were free. They had learned it the hard way––from stern experience. So when the British government tried to regiment them and obstruct their efforts, they simply ignored it. When the King laid down silly restrictions and controls on trade, the colonists went right on trading. When the weaving of cloth was prohibited in order to protect weavers in England, the women of America kept right on working at their looms."

The Unknown Individual

This tells of the unknown individuals who risked their lives for liberty—those whose actions led up to the Declaration of Independence. When the tentative document was ready, representatives from each colony met together to consider its adoption.

"These representatives were gentlemen of solid responsibility and high social position––including Benjamin Franklin, John Adams, Richard Henry Lee, Charles Carroll, Robert Morris, John Hancock, James Wilson, Roger Sherman, and George Walton. Such men had everything to gain by standing with the King. If they joined the rebels, they risked not only their own lives, but also the lives of their families. Under English law, their children and their children's children would be attainted traitors.

"Each man attending the meeting possessed a landed estate, a substantial business, a professional position––or all three. He need only do nothing. By keeping quiet, he might save his property, his superior class status, and his life. And he could easily justify his position on the premise that, while he might not wholly agree with the government's policies, a good subject's duty is to obey the laws and remain loyal to his king.

"Some of them refused to sign, and each man who did sign knew what he risked when he wrote his signature under the words: 'We mutually pledge to each other our Lives. . . .' He was prepared to lose his life when he signed a declaration of that ten-year-old war, its causes and its motives:

> 'We hold these truths to be self-evident, that all men are created equal, that they are endowed by their Creator with certain unalienable rights, that among these are Life, Liberty and the Pursuit of Happiness.'

"The Philadelphia group was undertaking not only to win the war, but to lay the groundwork for an entirely new kind of state. They were assuming leadership of the weak and losing side, and the problems were many. First of all, money would have to be raised, and the military effort would have to be better organized. Scattered mobs could never defeat Great Britain.

"The aspects were not bright. The King's troops were advancing down the Hudson River. His fleet was approaching New York. The leaders of the Revolution were faced with the armed might of the British Empire—with 13 disorganized and quarreling colonies at their backs."

The story continues with the dissension over the various state constitutions and the great dilemma over federation.

The New Model

"Another six years of confusion and discouragement followed the surrender of Cornwallis. The leaders of the Revolution were negotiating the peace treaty and trying to hold the Continental Congress together, to keep the States from fighting each other, and to figure out a way to pay something on the French debt before the French army moved in to collect it. During this period, when George Washington had less hope than at Valley Forge, the leaders of the Revolution made one last effort to unite the independent States.

"With the State constitutions as their guide, they attempted to write an over-all constitution which would combine the States into a co-operative federation, designed to work on the principles of individual freedom, liberty, and law.

"Common men were to run their own affairs. All persons were to have equal power so that each would be free to struggle for his own self-interest, in order to arrive at a satisfactory balance in his relationships with other men.

"The problem was not new. It was as old as history, but no one had ever found the answer. The Greeks had been unable to solve it. The Romans had been unable to solve it. Various experiments had been tried, and all had failed.

"No one had ever found the solution. But it is doubtful that, in the entire history of mankind, so unusual a group had ever come together for so important a purpose——realistic frontiersmen, practical builders, jurists, statesmen, students of history, analysts of Old World government from the perspective of a New World in the making. Their counterparts are rare in this modern age of specialization and so-called 'progressive' education.

"America was to be set up as a republic——which means that the laws would be made and administered by representatives chosen, directly and indirectly, by the people to protect the interests of all the people.

"The word *republic* means rule *for* the people, and as Isabel Peterson points out:

> 'A Republic signifies an organization dealing with affairs which concern the public, thus implying that there are also private affairs, a sphere of social and personal life, with which government is not and should not be concerned; it sets a limit to the political power.'

"In the last analysis, any government, regardless of what it may be called, must be one man or a small group of men in power over many men. The only way in which men can remain free and be left in control of their individual energies is to cut the power of government to an irreducible minimum.

"But how can that be done without the danger of out-and-out anarchy? The answer is quite simple——once it is found. But until the time of the American Revolution, no one had found it.

"The head of a State is a human being; and a human being's thinking, deciding, acting, and judging are inseparable. But in this new American republic, no top official would ever be permitted to act as a whole human being. The functions of government would be divided into three parts:

1. The first part was to think and decide. It would be called the *Congress*.

2. The second part was to be responsible for getting action. It would be headed by the chief executive––the *President*.
3. The third part was to serve as judge or referee and would be known as the *Supreme Court*.

Each of these three parts was to act as a check on the other two; and over the three was set a written statement of political principles, intended to be the strongest check on them all. There was to be government by law––with clearly defined rules of the game––rather than government by whim. Thus, the Constitution was to serve as an impersonal restraint upon the fallible human beings who must be allowed to use their fragments of authority over the multitudes of free individuals.

"The dangers of dictatorship must be avoided for all time to come. No one person nor small group of persons must ever be permitted to get too much power; and the minority––even down to the last individual citizen––must be protected against oppression by the majority or by any organized pressure group.

"Such were the objectives of the American revolutionary leaders, and for months they struggled to draw the blueprints for this new and completely different political structure.

"The federal government, along with state governments, county governments, and city governments, must be set up as the servant rather than as the master––and it must be kept that way.

"The first ten amendments were the 'price of ratification.' They guarantee freedom of speech, freedom of the press, religious freedom, and the right of trial by jury. In addition, public officials are forbidden to seize or to search a person or his property or his private papers––except under certain definite circumstances prescribed by written law. Private property cannot be taken for public use without just compensation to its owner. Cruelty is outlawed once and for all, and any accused person is to be considered innocent until his guilt is proven.

"And last, but not least, it became a part of constitutional law that any powers not specifically granted to the Federation automatically remain in the hands of the separate states or in the hands of the people themselves.

"Thus the individual's life, liberty, and property rights are to be held secure against unjust acts, not only on the part of other individuals, but also on the part of the government itself.

"These early amendments are known collectively as the 'Bill of Rights,' but the name is misleading and tends to confuse a careless mind.

"The word *rights* reflects the feudal concept. It is entirely accurate as used in England because the English 'bill of rights' is a statement of certain freedoms which the British government *permits* its subjects.

"But in America, it's exactly the opposite. Our so-called Bill of Rights is really a statement of prohibitions, and it defines the uses of force that will or will not be granted to public officials. It is based on the principle that human rights are natural rights––born in every human being along with his life––and are inseparable from life itself. People cannot be given that which already belongs to them––and only to them.

"Here, in America, men in public office were to be the recipients, not the donors, of permission. They were to be the servants, not the masters, of the people.

"That is what makes the American concept of constitutional government different from that of the British government or that of any other government that had ever gone before. This difference is the essence, the very foundation, of the revolution. Ours is the only basic innovation of political structure since the beginning of recorded history.

"That's an important point to remember––especially during these hectic times when the Old World 'isms', after a bit of facelifting and re-labeling, are being presented in glowing terms as something entirely new and ultra-modern. The safety, the freedom, the security, the very life of every American and the future of his children depend upon our understanding the meaning of the *real* revolution."

Unplanned Planning

"The states had united in a voluntary federation, but there was no unified control, no over-all plan.

"This is just the opposite of the Old World pattern. In other nations, the overlords develop their ambitious plans, enforced by the firing squad and supported by huge predatory armies. These plans look fine on paper, but they are contradictory to the nature of human energy. They are always at the expense of individual initiative; they always result in oppression, leading to human degradation and war.

"In America, the planning was to be done on a decentralized, or grass-roots basis. It was a new experiment. Free men were to have an opportunity to live their lives, plan their own affairs, and work with one another——not under the lash of coercive authority, but under the discipline of enlightened self-interest and moral responsibility.

"Thus it is that Americans were assured the flexibilities necessary to progress. Thus it is that always in these United States the unintended, the unpredictable, the apparently irrational has seemed to carry us forward."

Weaver then cites as examples the settlement of Kentucky, which seemed against the general welfare (and which soon forced the Louisiana Purchase) and the almost personal adventure of General Fremont which took California from Mexico.

"Everywhere you look in American history, you find examples of things seeming to happen by accident——without intention. Americans had no over-all plan. They had something more important. They had personal freedom to plan their own affairs; and the avalanche of human energy resulting from that freedom swept from the Atlantic to the Pacific, from the Great Lakes to the Rio Grande.

"The whole vast extent of this country had been covered by one nation, a tumultuous multitude of free men——men of heterogeneous races and creeds——living under the weakest government in the world. The people who had been left to shift for themselves——who had learned the lessons of realism and learned them the hard way——were creating a new world and carrying forward the revolution which was beginning to shake the foundations of the Old World."

The Revolution Spreads

"'An army of principles,' declared Thomas Paine, 'will penetrate where an army of soldiers cannot; it will succeed where diplomatic management would fail; it is neither the Rhine, the Channel, nor the ocean that can arrest its progress; it will march on the horizon of the world, and it will conquer.'

"Many Europeans had joined the Americans during the war, and they carried home the sentiments of Paine––as well as the sentiments of Lafayette, who said: 'For a nation to love liberty, it is sufficient that she knows it.'

"And there were converts among the mercenary soldiers who had been brought over from Europe to fight for Britain. Many of them were coming to the same conclusion as the captured Hessian who confided to Paine: 'America is a fine, free country . . . I know the difference by knowing my own; in my country, if the Prince says, "eat straw", we eat straw.' The sentiment for freedom was spreading.

"The initial effort met with reverses, but the new revolution––the *real* revolution––was on the march. During the period 1810-1812, it spread southward in the Western world. There were revolts in Mexico, Venezuela, Argentina, Chile, Paraguay, and Uruguay. In 1813 Mexico declared its independence from Spain; and in 1819, the people of Columbia took the same action."

PART IV   FRUITS OF FREEDOM

Inventive Progress

"When the American revolution had its beginning, living conditions had scarcely changed since the reign of Nebuchadnezzar. The colonial woman gathered her own firewood and cooked over an open fire, just as women had cooked since the dawn of history, and just as more than two-thirds of the women on earth are cooking today. She spun thread and wove coarse cloth, with a spindle and loom handed down from the early Egyptians. Every housewife made her own soap and candles and

41

carried water from a spring or well. A crude millstone, dating back to ancient Babylon, ground the grain that the American farmer cut and threshed with knives and flails that were older than history.

"These were the conditions existing when our forefathers threw off the shackles of Old World tyranny in order that human beings might be in control of their own lives and make full use of their individual initiative.

"The outburst of human energy was terrific, and in no way is it better illustrated than by the inventive progress that immediately took place."

Weaver outlines the fascinating story of inventions from steam engines to steamboats, pins and nails, plows to reaper and combine. He discusses the value to society of these inventions and shows that any amount given the inventor was negligible in comparison.

"In addition to the cotton gin, the modern steamboat, the prairie sodbuster, the reaper, and the binder, Americans invented the sewing machine, the typewriter, the linotype, the telegraph, the telephone, the phonograph, the motion picture, the airplane, the washing machine, the electric refrigerator, and dozens of other electrical appliances.

"And Americans developed the techniques of quantity production. In a broad, over-all sense, one might argue that mass production, as we know it in this country, is the most important of all inventions because it is only through mass production that the practical benefits of other inventions can be extended to the millions.

"But mass production rests on the foundation of another, and an even greater invention. It is our new and original concept of a political structure based on a principle that is just as true, just as real, just as inexorable as any law of physics——the principle of *individual liberty and freedom*, the principle that each person controls his own life-energy and is responsible for his own acts and for his relationships with others.

"This, the first and foremost of all our inventive contributions, is not ordinarily thought of as an invention. But the fact remains that it is the greatest of them all because it serves as the foundation for all the others and provides the opportunity for their full fruition."

Hope Versus Fear

"Inventions and discoveries were being made in the Old World long before the White Man came to America. They are still being made, and they will continue to be made by the few unsquelchable geniuses who, in spite of the static surroundings, persist in their independent thinking––without much hope of reward unless the brain child has military possibilities.

"But when creative workers find themselves entangled in artificial restrictions and bureaucratic red tape––in addition to the natural, normal and unavoidable difficulties surrounding their work––much of the potential talent will die on the vine. There must be opportunities and incentives to invent and opportunities and incentives to use; and in between, there must be opportunities and incentives to produce and exchange. Here in America, such opportunities and incentives have been more far-reaching and more favorable than anywhere else in the world.

"The only sound program for free competitive enterprise––the only program that has a chance to succeed––is one which concerns itself, first, last and always, with maintaining freedom for the individual citizen––let the chips fall where they may. It's a matter of keeping the way open so that any business or trade group, large or small, may be continually challenged, kept on its toes, even put out of business, by any runner-up who can demonstrate an ability to serve the customer better.

"It may be argued, and it frequently is, that free competition is a ruthless and cruel process. But it is not nearly so ruthless and cruel as the opposite philosophy, which down through the ages has kept the majority of people ill-fed, ill-housed, ill-clothed, embroiled in wars, and dying of famine and pestilence.

"There is no escaping the fact that human effort is motivated by hope of reward on the one hand, and by fear of punishment on the other. The ideal combination is rewards that are great and reasonably attainable and punishments that are not too severe.

"America's economic progress is the result of conditions which have provided maximum opportunities for reward, but which have limited the penalties to personal insecurity and business bankruptcy. At the other extreme is the totalitarian state, which promises security at the expense of freedom and which attempts to 'encourage' initiative by the threat of the concentration camp or firing squad.

"Under free competition based on personal responsibility and voluntary cooperation, our production of useful goods and services has exceeded anything ever before accomplished. The big point is that our progress to date is the result of an entirely new and different form of political structure which made it possible for human energy and individual initiative to work under their own natural control.

"The inventive mind is an inquiring mind, and the inquiring mind is the mind of a doubter and challenger. Creative thinkers are never satisfied to let well enough alone. They are continually straying off the beaten path and getting out of step with normal routine. Such people have no place in an authoritarian society. Even though their explorations may be confined to the area of physical things, there's always the danger of their turning up something that might disturb the planned economy and discredit the superior wisdom of the overlords.

"Inventive and scientific talent of a high degree can't be produced by bureaucratic edict. Nor can it be discovered through any formalized procedure––the only way it can be done is through *natural selection*. In other words, let the creative mind discover itself. That's the only effective process, and it can only be fully effective in an atmosphere which doesn't prevent anyone from using his own initiative.

"The greater the competition, the better the quality of the persons who reach the top. This is due, not only to the greater number of aspirants, but also to the fact that genius thrives on rivalry. It's not much fun to be an expert in a field which is completely and entirely beyond the understanding of everyone else.

"In the last analysis, all of these advantages are the natural, normal outgrowth of a political structure which unleashed the creative energy of millions of men and women by leaving them free to work out their own affairs––not under the lash of coercive authority, but through voluntary co-operation based on enlightened self-interest and moral responsibility."

Moral Versus Material

"The third attempt to set men free has made the great grand-children of the revolutionary leaders the best-fed, the best-clothed, the best-housed, and the most prosperous people on the face of the globe. Many of the things that we have come to take for granted as commonplace necessities of life would have been beyond the fondest dreams of luxury-seeking kings and potentates a few years ago.

"America's outstanding progress in the realm of material things is the result of an approach which was based on sound moral principles; which threw aside the pagan superstition of a static universe; and which admitted no limitations to man's progress so long as he directs his imaginative abilities and creative faculties in harmony with truth and rightness.

"In the static world of the pagans, the only way to gain a benefit was to take something away from someone else. Under that philosophy, human energy which might have been used to increase wealth was always wasted in fighting over existing wealth. This went on for thousands upon thousands of years; in the process, material wealth was destroyed, human energy was dissipated, and desolation prevailed.

"Then, here in America, after 160 years of voluntary co-operation between free individuals, we have pointed the way to a world of peace and plenty. Although we've just barely reached the threshold, we've gone far enough to disprove the age-old superstition that for one person to make a profit, the other must suffer a loss. Under the American formula, the soundness of the Golden Rule becomes increasingly apparent; and for the first time in history, we have witnessed the paradox of higher wages, lower prices, more things for more people—and we're only just getting started!

"It is true that America is far from perfect; and being a self-critical and progressive people, we find it easy to visualize a much better world. But in admitting our shortcomings and laying our plans to overcome them, there are three questions which might well be asked:

1. To what degree are our shortcomings traceable to the form of political structure under which our country was founded?

2. To what degree are they due to our having drifted away from the concept?
3. How does our record compare with the records of countries which have tried to operate under the opposite philosophy?

And in drawing comparisons, it's important to bear in mind that we've been at it less than 200 years, as against thousands of years of experience with various forms of regimentation.

"Today we hear a lot of talk to the effect that our original form of government has been outmoded; that it's old-fashioned and needs to be brought up to date; that you can't resist the trend of history; and that we are now in the midst of a new world-revolution.

"But the truth of the matter is that the American revolution for human freedom is the only thing that's really new, and it did not end with the surrender of Cornwallis nor with the signing of the Constitution. It's still going on, and the counter-revolutionists––the enemies of freedom––are on the march. Their major attack is not on the open battlefield. It is in the fifth-column technique of skillfully boring from within––a program of infiltration and attrition.

"The principal secret weapon is traceable to Lenin, who allegedly instructed his followers to first confuse the vocabulary. Lenin was smart. He knew that thinking can be done only in words and that accurate thinking requires words of precise meaning. Confuse the vocabulary, and the unsuspecting majority is at a disadvantage when defending themselves against the small but highly disciplined minority which knows exactly what it wants and which deliberately promotes word-confusion as the first step in its efforts to divide and conquer.

"Offhand, one would assume that free Americans, with their unprecedented record of progress, would be completely immune to the propaganda of those who advocate a reversion to pagan ideology. But paradoxically, people who have lived their lives in a civilization founded on Christian ethics are at a serious disadvantage when defending themselves against the surreptitious tactics of those who deny all moral values and who are obsessed with the immoral fallacy, *the end justifies the means.*

"We in America are up against the problem of protecting ourselves against the jujitsu tactics of those who would have us commit suicide by using our own strength to destroy the very things which are responsible for that strength. Without regard for moral principles of decency and fair play, their techniques are skillfully designed to take advantage of our virtues and to turn them into weaknesses.

"Our habit of self-criticism, which is largely responsible for our progress, makes us particularly vulnerable to distorted propaganda which exaggerates our deficiencies and holds out false promises of a short cut to the millennium. Thus it is that some of our most patriotic, high-minded, and well-meaning citizens succumb to the overtures of those who would make them the innocent tools of subversion.

"The fact that we are a progressive and open-minded people, always on the alert for new ideas, makes us susceptible to old ideas when they are attractively camouflaged and presented as something new.

"Being a hospitable, tolerant, and fair-minded people, we are inclined to consider both sides of every question. That's all right up to a point, *but when it comes to the eternal verities of moral truth, there are no two sides to the question.* Right is right, and wrong is wrong; and any concession to the pagan viewpoint—whether in the name of expediency or open-mindedness—paves the way for the destruction of all moral values.

"With the shortest working hours on earth, we have greater opportunities for self-improvement and personal advancement. But please note that the emphasis is on the word *opportunities.* The matter of taking advantage of opportunities is up to the individual. It cannot be otherwise. *There are no substitutes for self-faith, self-reliance, self-development, individual effort, and personal responsibility.* Life is no bed of roses. *The end of man is not self-indulgence, but achievement.* There are no short cuts, no substitutes for work.

"Human life came into being and aspires to advance in the face of conflict, struggle, pain, and death. In the last analysis, no person's security can exceed his own self-reliance; when anyone denies this self-evident truth, the chances are that he has for too long depended on someone else to do his fighting for him.

"Living is a tough job. Only good fighters can make a go of it. The tragedy is that we waste our energies in fighting one another, instead of fighting the common enemies of mankind––famine, pestilence, disease, and other destructive forces of the nonhuman world."

Freedom Versus War

"Under the pagan fallacy of a static universe in which new wealth cannot be created, the only way to gain an advantage is to take something away from someone else. When men are free, they soon learn that wars of aggression are unprofitable; that human energies are far more productive when applied to the peaceful pursuits of creating and exchanging useful goods and services.

"Down through the ages, human beings have always tried to stop war by utterly crushing the enemy. There has been no progress, for the simple reason that the underlying cause of war is *not* the enemy. Combat on the battlefield is merely a symptom. War is caused by a false notion of human energy, now based on the ancient superstition that men and women should be reduced to the status of the beehive. When the majority of people on this earth come to realize that they are free, self-controlling, responsible for their own acts and for their relationships with others, there will be no war.

CHAPTER

IV

WHY WAGES RISE

The fateful delayed reversal in social reactions, like an obscure puzzle, becomes quite obvious when all steps are clearly presented. An excellent primer for this purpose, with regard to economic problems, is the essay by F. A. Harper[1] entitled *Why Wages Rise*. The following condensation of a few sentences from his introduction outlines the problem: "Wages are of prime importance in any advanced economy such as ours. There is evidence aplenty that the economic principles which apply to wage problems are not well understood, no better now than in the early thirties when measures adopted to combat the depression proved to

---

[1] Dr. Harper (Ph.D., Cornell 1932) taught Economics and Marketing at Cornell and other universities, served as research field agent and business analyst for the U.S. Government, was with FEE (The Foundation for Economic Education, Irvington-On-Hudson, N.Y.) for many years and is now president of the unique Institute for Humane Studies, Menlo Park, Calif. (See page 206) Among many honors bestowed upon Dr. Harper are Life Fellow of the International Institute of Arts and Letters (Switzerland) and Fellow of the American Association for the Advancement of Science. A few of his many writings are: *Crisis of the Free Economy; Liberty: A Path to its Recovery; Inflation; Morals and the Welfare State; Sequoyah: Symbol of Free Men; Gaining the Free Market.* He has contributed articles to many professional, journals and to *The Freeman*[2] *as well as a most interesting essay to the symposium (written in honor of Ludwig von Mises) On Freedom and Free Enterprise.*[3] *Why Wages Rise* was published by FEE in 1957.

be such colossal failure[2] . . . . We now seem enmeshed in chronic and progressive inflation which Lenin once said was a sure and simple way to destroy the capitalist system. Our prosperity will surely end in the destruction of capitalism unless we can resolve this problem which in a large measure is a wage problem.

"I shall deal with the wage problem in a manner that may seem oversimplified. Basic principles always have a way of seeming simple. Yet if they be principles, they can no more be oversimplified than the law of gravity. What is needed in our complex society is to get back to simple economic principles. They are working tools for solving problems that seem more complex than they really are."

Harper continues by discussing two major roadblocks which obstruct a thorough insight into the wage problem. The primary block is the general lack of understanding of the difference, in a changing economy, between money wages and real wages. This lack aggravates the widespread misunderstanding of the true effect of unions upon real wages and this misunderstanding constitutes the second big roadblock.

"When speaking of wages and what makes them rise, the meaning will be the over-all level of wages––the general welfare, in that sense. To speak otherwise of wages, such as wage rates for one or a few persons, would involve special situations which are not the object of this discussion. A bank robber might succeed in gaining a high wage for his hour of work; a few persons, through power and special privilege, might likewise gain some short-time advantages at the expense of the others who work. But such gains of some wage earners are not the aim or meaning of this analysis of why wages rise."

The first chapters are merely mentioned as the material is more fully reviewed in Chapter V.

1. LABOR UNIONS

---

[2] Two excellent books on this subject are: *America's Great Depression* by Murray Rothbard, which gives a thorough exposition of *what* wrong measures brought on and deepened the depression, and *The Peoples Pottage* by Garet Garrett, which includes a penetrating analysis of *why* the depression was so extensive.

This chapter gives the history of wage rates and unionization from 1850 to 1955 and shows clearly that unionization had no possible effect toward increasing real wages. Harper concludes with: "And so this popular illusion that rising wages are due to the growth of labor unions must be discarded if there is to be any room for attention to other possible causes.

"As a preview to the answer as to what makes wages rise, I will merely say here that wages can be paid only out of what is produced. Something other than your joining a union is what increased your hourly economic output––now five times that of your great-grandfather's a century ago."

If, after reading here the condensations of Harper and Hazlitt, there is the slightest doubt as to the correctness of this conclusion it is suggested that both books be read in their entirety, and if necessary that other referenced works also be studied.

2. PRODUCTIVITY

This analysis starts with the obvious truth that consumption cannot exceed production whether for one isolated pioneer or for millions of people. It continues with data showing that real wages per hour have kept very close to product produced per hour.

3. DIVIDING THE PIE

Personal income is divided into the two basic elements: Pay for work done currently, and pay for the use of savings––ie, income from work done in the past and not used for consumption at that time. The ratio is about 6 to 1––only about 15% going to those whose savings provide the tools which do some 95% of the work. Thus if all profit was diverted to wages the increase would be about the same as normally occurs in approximately six years––but without the profit there could be no new tools and soon there would be no jobs and no wages at all.

The fallacies of slavery and of the Labor and Surplus Value theories are analyzed––to the conclusion that ". . . today, being as dependent as we are on tools, the surplus value theory is a sort of economic bomb which, if infused into action, could do unbelievable damage.

"The problem of dividing the pie should be left to the free market of individual choices among employees and employers; consumers and producers, investors and borrowers; traders of all sorts, everywhere in exchange.

"Wherever the pie is divided by the free market, one thing seems sure: Marx's surplus value theory will be vetoed. For persons will continue, as they have over the past few centuries in our relatively free United States, to recognize a bargain when they see one. That bargain is tools. Of our total output, perhaps as much as 95% is because of the use of tools. And this at a cost of only about 15% of total output, as pay to those who have saved to create these tools. That, and not Marx's concept, is the miracle that creates a surplus of value."

4. TOOLS TO HARNESS ENERGY

The amounts and efficiencies of various types of animal and mechanical energy are outlined and a table shows that the ratio of mechanical to human power has increased over five times since 1850 and that this is the reason that real wages also increased approximately five times.

5. DOING WHAT YOU CAN DO BEST

Covers the seeming miracle of specialization—highly skilled workers with special tools producing vast quantities of quality products at low cost. The necessity for specialization, and its limitations, are carefully analyzed.

6. THE LUBRICANT FOR EXCHANGE

Harper calls money the greatest economic invention of all time as it lubricates the vast economic mechanism of trade which could not operate without it. He tells of the various items historically used for money and describes how inflation is similar to adding counterfeit money. He analyzes the effect of inflation on wages and concludes that it would be a major disaster; "My final point is to suggest the disaster that would come upon us if, through inflation and deflation, the efficiency of the lubricant for exchange should be retarded, or the money system destroyed. What if violent changes should turn money from a lubricant into an object of speculation? For when persons hoard money in anticipation that it will gain worth, this miraculous lubricant cannot do its work. Then catastrophe would be upon our highly geared economy. Then the usual progress which causes real wages to rise could no longer operate, until and unless a new lubricant were found and installed.

"We are interested here in why wages rise, in a real sense rather than in an illusory sense. It behooves all of us who want continued progress, therefore, to become greatly concerned about this threat of inflation. This means searching out the underlying cause of why governments either want to inflate money or feel impelled to do so, then correcting the cause."

7. CONTRACTING FOR PROGRESS

This chapter analyzes the inflationary effect of wage contracts which include scheduled increases, especially increases tied to the rising cost-of-living index. It includes a chart which shows how wage rates have increased from a base of 100 in 1910 to nearly 800 in 1955 while purchasing ability increased to less than 300—the 500 difference being due to inflation. The concluding paragraphs summarize as follows: "In speaking of the consequences of inflation at the time of the French Revolution, Andrew Dickson White said:

'Now began to be seen more plainly some of the many ways in which an inflation policy robs the working class . . . the classes living on fixed incomes and small salaries felt the pressure first, as soon as the purchasing power of their fixed incomes was reduced. Soon the great class living on wages felt it even more sadly . . . the

53

> demand for labor was diminished; laboring men were
> thrown out of employment . . . the price of labor . . .
> went down . . . Workmen of all sorts were more and
> more thrown out of employment."[3]

"So if the wage earner is to be able to enjoy further increases in *real* wages through a healthy and sound economic growth, inflation must be stopped. But inflation can never be stopped if it becomes entrenched in the wage structure as a contractual way of life. It can never be stopped if wage contracts are so designed that employers and employees come to have a divided and conflicting interest in meeting the common enemy of inflation.

"Progress cannot be built on an inflation bubble. It cannot be built on a raise in wages offset by a decline in what a dollar of wage will buy. For then the welfare of the wage earners will burst when the inflation bubble bursts, hurting them especially."

Inflation is the increase in money—rising prices are only a result. Inflation is impossible with a free economy on a gold standard but it is almost a certainty in a welfare state off the gold standard. Creeping inflation can continue for considerable time until the general public finally awakens to the fact that money continually depreciates in value. Then it tends to become "galloping" inflation which can avalanche as in China and Germany. German monetary value fell such that *ten billion dollars* original equivalent in 1918 ended as worth approximately *one U.S. cent* some five years later.[4]

8. THE COST OF BEING GOVERNED

This chapter starts with an extreme analogy which clearly illustrated that taxes are a forced expense and "that if you are forced to buy certain

---

[3] Andrew Dixon White, *Fiat Money Inflation in France*, FEE, 1952.

[4] A German history book, *Um Volksstaat und Volkergemeinshaft*, published by Ernst Klett, Stuttgart 1961, page 149, lists prices of a number of common foods from 1914 to 1923. A fair average rise from 1918 to 1923 is *one trillion times*. A pound of butter ranged from 1.5 marks in 1914 to 3 marks in 1918 to 2400 in 1922 to 150,000 in Summer 1923 to 6,000,000,000,000 in November 1923.

'goods' or a 'service' priced by edict, you are an enslaved buyer." He analyzes the various value relationships and gives a chart of buying power from 1860 and 1955 which shows the heavy portion taken by taxes.

The startling but obvious conclusion is that since wage earners cannot force real wages higher than production increases, they should concentrate on reduction in cost of government. This is shown by the following excerpts: "The present cost of governing ourselves (cost of government) is about 31 times as much as it was a century ago, per person, and aside from the effect of inflation on dollar cost.

"In closing, I would emphatically suggest that perhaps the best way to get higher wages now would be to hire out to ourselves individually, so to speak, for more of the job of governing ourselves. That would mean more self-reliance, more self-control, and all the rest. In this way great savings could be made in the drain on our incomes, leaving that much more to spend on things of our choice and preference. This, in effect, is the same thing as a rise in wages.

"Those of us who labor for a living might well consider a completely new direction––a new objective––in our bargaining for wages. Since there is no more to be gotten from employers than the slow increase in productivity will allow, perhaps we should start directing our bargaining power at government. Why not govern ourselves more, and thereby be able to keep more of what we are nominally paid? A dollar saved is a dollar earned."

9. LOSING PAY THROUGH FRINGE BENEFITS

"When you can't use your income for things of your choice, its worth is lessened for you.

"The greatest opportunity now for a quick increase in the worth of wages is to reduce the cost of governing ourselves so that more of the wage can be kept.

"But there is another aspect of free choice in the spending of wages, by which it is possible to raise the worth of wages even further.

"The communists-socialists have a plan for society that goes like this: 'From each according to his ability, *to each according to his need.*'

"This communal blueprint is appealing enough on the surface. Each of us wants to do the best he can according to his ability. And who among us doesn't yearn to have his needs fulfilled? So this slogan sounds like Heaven before the hereafter.

"The barb in the bait lies concealed beneath the pleasant dreams of a utopia. For the brutal discipline of reality rules over hopes that can't be hatched.

"The catch is twofold. First, as a member of a communist-socialist society you shall not be allowed the privilege of pursuing the release of your abilities at a task which seems best to you. A central authority will decide this for you and for everyone else.

"The second catch in this slogan is that your official allotment 'according to need' will have no necessary relationship to your hopes and expectations. For it is the central authority, not you, who decides on your needs. And so the Heaven of your dreams turns to a sorrowful reality."

Harper ties this concept with our present trend toward "fringe" benefits and shows that these are a form of forced saving for things which likely are not most wanted and thus not worth the cost. He calls these "Fringe Detriments."

"Most schemes of this sort are not really benefits at all. Employees would be better off, by their standards of need, if they could have the money instead. Then they could buy something worth more to them than any common package, more than any communized 'need' that could be devised.

"My dictionary says that the opposite of a benefit is a detriment. So instead of being a fringe benefit, these kinds of things are really *fringe detriments.* Even then, they are not on the fringe of your welfare; they are as much at the heart of your welfare as any other dollar of your pay."

So-called fringe benefits in 1955 comprised 10 to 20% of wages and were increasing rapidly so a prompt and substantial wage raise can be obtained by eliminating all fringe detriments. By giving each worker his full wage he could then spend his money as he preferred, and if certain workers desired a "package deal" they could obtain it on the market without penalizing the other workers who did not want it.

"The worth of wages can in this way be raised at once, anywhere employers and employees decide to do so. It need not wait the slow process of increasing productivity. In fact, this is necessary if we are to gain the full benefits possible under our increased capacity to produce."

A Freeze on Opportunity

"And as a final point, these schemes of so-called fringe benefits often are a serious threat to our continued progress. Ostensibly their purpose is to reduce the turnover of labor and stabilize employment. But they tend to freeze a worker in his job. He does not leave for a more productive job because he would then lose his seniority status and the 'accumulated benefits' which he cannot take with him. So he keeps his 'security,' which the union or the company allows him to have only if he stays where he is. He does not follow opportunity where it leads. This sort of freezing tends back toward the old European caste system, and could bring an end to the traditional American growth of welfare and increasing wages.

"So 'fringe benefits,' rather than coming from pie in the sky, come out of wages—out of what could be paid as money wages. And, furthermore, they comprise a serious threat to our progress."

10. LEISURE AND THE BETTER LIFE

The various uses of vacation and leisure time are outlined and it is shown that an average worker can now exist on about one-tenth of the working time required a century ago. The time actually worked is reduced to only about one-half and the difference allows for our greatly increased standard of living. A chart shows the U.S. Productive Capacity from 1855 to 1955 and also the reduction due to increased leisure.

Our highly tooled economy has so raised productive capacity that now we have the pleasant choice of more total income or more leisure.

Harper shows that unions have had negligible effect on total hours of work and that they are foolish to make such a claim.

"One cannot know for sure, of course, what the length of the work week would now be in the absence of unions. But let us assume that in the absence of unions we would now be working more hours—that unions have, in other words, reduced the work week beyond the free choice of individual workers. If that were the case, the attainment would amount to a disservice to the wage earners. For we would then have to conclude that the workers, under union pressure, have been forced to accept leisure—fewer work hours—instead of their preference for somewhat more hours and increased buying power."

Vacations with pay are shown to be only an accounting device: "It is clear that there can't be idleness with pay unless there is at some other time an equal amount of work without pay. 'Vacations with pay' are an accounting device only. They are really vacations without pay, no matter when and how the pay checks are arranged during the year." School teachers are a perfect example—most districts establish a yearly salary and some allow the individual teacher to choose payment in 9, 10 or 12 monthly installments.

Looking to the Future

"If the uptrend in our productive capacity continues as in the past, we shall be able to continue to choose between more leisure and more economic things. How far leisure may eventually go, we have no way of knowing. Automation and atomic power hold untold possibilities of this sort, unless a loss of liberty should terminate progress."

Harper then discusses the problem of increasing leisure and notes that it tends to corrode both virtue and wisdom. Work not only keeps people out of mischief, time-wise, but it also seems to have a direct therapeutic value on virtue and "its substitute under leisure seems not yet to have been found."

"For instance, in my files is evidence from capable authorities pointing out that the shorter work week is an important cause of crime; . . . that compulsory unemployment devices, such as child labor laws coupled with required presence in school buildings during teen-age years, are important causes of juvenile delinquency.

"Mental problems of all sorts, too, may in some important degree be the product of increasing leisure.

"The paradox of all this is that it may be the problems which leisure brings that will, in the future, offer unlimited opportunities for work in solving them.

"So in conclusion, increased productivity has gone more and more into leisure in preference to a more sumptuous life. As a result, yearly wages are not nearly as high as they could be if we had not prized the leisure more, if we had not chosen it instead. But having once made the choice this way, leisure itself creates serious problems which are suggested without being resolved."

11. PRICING AN HOUR OF WORK

Proper pricing is the crux of the whole book, so we shall use more condensed direct quotes.

"The general level of real wages is determined by what is produced. Inflating pay beyond this point raises prices but does not raise the worth of the wage in buying power. Unions, with all their political and other power, cannot veto the iron ceiling that production sets over real wages.

"The lone pioneer's desire for some meat, some wheat, or a log cabin is the incentive which drives him to produce. Anticipating his future wants, he produces in advance, like a squirrel which gathers and stores nuts for winter. And in anticipation of years of future use, he makes himself some tools to aid in his labors and in the enjoyment of living.

"Then having produced these things, the pioneer is his own sole market. In this situation there is no pricing problem because there is no money and no exchange. Nothing remains unsold as a result of the seller setting his price too high."

Production Creates Own Market

"But we are not lone pioneers. We live, instead, in a complex economy. A person usually produces a specialty, selling most of it to many persons and buying his varied needs from many other persons.

"Even so, the over-all situation is the same as for the lone pioneer to the extent that no more can be bought then is produced. Despite the fact that some goods and services are exchanged for others, and despite the fact that money may be used to facilitate these exchanges, what is bought still equals what is sold. Just as in one exchange the buying equals the selling because the same item sold by one person is bought by another, so likewise for the total of all trade in a complex economy, all buying equals all selling.

"And this leads to the unavoidable conclusion that *production creates its own buying power in a free economy*. Sales equal purchases and purchases equal sales, in total for all trade as for a single trade."

The Function of A Free Price

"The function of a free price is to accomplish in a complex economy of exchanges what the lone pioneer accomplishes in his separate existence––the production of what is wanted of each thing, and no more, insofar as is possible. The function of price is to discourage production of unwanted items and to encourage production of what is wanted, to the extent that wants can be anticipated and production plans can be carried out.

"The lone pioneer has his own troubles in this respect, of course. Perhaps the fishing is not as good as he had expected, or the weather not good for the corn. Perhaps in winter he changes his mind about what he wants, wishing he had provided more venison and less corn. Or perhaps his wife wishes the cabin had been fixed up a little, even if it had meant less hunting. Or perhaps too much food was stored and some of it spoiled. What does he do then? He just blames himself for his lack of foresight and adjusts as promptly as possible.

"In a complex economy, similar events occur. But one person can blame another more easily for not having foreseen the weather, or for the change in his wife's wants, or something of the sort. But the objectives of everyone in a complex society should be the same as if he were a lone pioneer––to adjust as promptly as possible and go on with production and living. That is the task performed by prices that are free."

A simple but important chart clearly illustrates the effect of shifting price above or below the free market value.

"Two forces operate to create a surplus as prices are forced above the free market point––consumers want less and producers bring out more. And conversely, these two forces operate to create a shortage as prices are forced downward.

"And finally, as to the function of a free price, it will be noted that trading will be greatest at the equality point, a free price. Either above or below that point trading is lessened, either because things are not wanted at a higher price or because they will not be produced and made available at a lower price.

"So if we accept the fact that economic welfare is at its best when willing trading is at its greatest, we must also conclude the economic welfare is greater at the free market price than at any other point. If prices are forced away from the point of the free price in either direction, that destroys economic welfare."

Wages Are A Price

"The purpose of discussing the function of price in this detail is because a wage is a price, too. It is the price of doing work, just as the price of a bushel of wheat is the price for that embodiment of economic service. In both instances the owner––in one case the owner of the wheat and in the other case the owner of his own time and effort––is entering the market with something to sell. And buyers who want either the wheat or the work enter the market to buy and thus satisfy their respective wants.

"The laborer as a person is not a commodity in either instance, but the time of one and the product of the labors of the other are items of sale––both in a like sense.

"A worker may work for himself producing some product he sells on the market. Or he may sell his productive services to another person, who in turn sells the product on the market. Or he may work at some task like that of a household servant.

Since wages are a price, they are subject to all the rules of prices and pricing, the same as anything else. All that has been said about the function of price applies to wages the same as to wheat. There is a point of equality at the free market price where the supply of labor and the demand for labor find a balance. And there is no other point of wage-price where this is true.

"As wages are forced either above or below the free market point, there will be created either a surplus or a shortage of labor. And there will be less employment either above or below the free wage point––less labor traded––to the extent that higher wages discourage those who might want to employ help, whereas lower wages discourage people from wanting available jobs. In one direction from the free price, employers offer fewer and fewer jobs; in the other direction, fewer and fewer persons want jobs."

Bargaining for A Wage

"Bargaining over wages should have no other purpose, in terms of economic welfare, than to find the free market price for the labor involved. For that is the only price of labor where there is economic equality. It is the only price of labor where employment will be a maximum.

"How can one know whether the free market price has been found? So far as I can see, this can be judged only after the fact, on the basis of consequences. If other employers want you at a price you are getting, or perhaps more, your price on your services is too low. If, on the other hand, nobody wants you at the price you ask, your price is too high. And here as with the price of sweet corn, this figure of a free-price wage for yourself has nothing to do with the cost of producing you; it doesn't even have anything to do with your cost of living, which you adjust to your income rather than vice versa."

Unemployment

"When wheat is priced above the free market level, the accumulation that is unsalable at that price is called a *surplus*. When the comparable situation arises among the working force of a nation, we call it *unemployment*. This refers to the labor––perfectly good labor––which is going unsold at the wage-price.

"The only way there can ever really be a surplus of labor, unwanted at the price, is by some sort of force being used on wages to keep them above the free market price. It couldn't happen otherwise. The demand for labor is not a fixed thing. There is not an unchanging number of persons wanted for work. The number demanded depends on the wage."

The Demand for Labor

(Sen.) Paul H. Douglas, in his notable book *The Theory of Wages*, analyzes the effect of wage ratio and concludes that employment varies three to four times as much as wages. "That is, a decline of one per cent in wages would uncover jobs for three or four per cent more work. And vice versa."

This relationship is illustrated by a curve which shows that:

"Wages about 10% above the free market price would mean unemployment of about one-fourth of the working force.

"If wages were to go up about 26%, it would unemploy about half the working force."

According to this study, overemployment (negative unemployment) would result from too low a wage rate but such a condition can occur only on rare occasions, such as a war when persons not normally in the working force are induced to work for patriotic reasons.

12. RIDING THE WAVES OF BUSINESS

This concluding chapter reviews the factors which control employment and shows how total wages (all money earned by all workers) *drops* when wage rates exceed the free market value. A chart showing unemployment from 1900 to 1955 illustrates the relative balance of wages except during the depression years of 1930-41 "when unemployment rose to tremendous height—to as much as one-third of the number employed, at the peak in 1933. This indicates that there was a serious overpricing of wages during the 1930's.

"Wages need not be far out of line on a percentage basis to cause even that degree of unemployment, however. On the basis of the three-to-one leverage, for instance, a wage rate only about 10% too high could have caused that much unemployment."

The Danger of Controlled Wages

"It is clear from this evidence that the conclusions of Douglas . . . as to the elasticity of wages found confirmation in the tragic experience of the 1930's. It also shows that those who play with wage rates at the bargaining tables are toying with dynamite, not only as it endangers the worker's job but also his yearly income.

"It is clear, too, that those who play politically with wage controls are also playing with dynamite. The bitter experience of the thirties illustrates their chronic tendency to play their hand upside down, to the disadvantage of the presumed beneficiaries. Believing that nobody could want their income reduced, they use their power to the full to prevent wage rates from dropping. And the 'buying power' theory comes to their assistance at such times, by which it is argued that incomes must be kept up if consumers are to be enabled to buy back the things they have produced. (See footnote on page 66.)

"But keeping income up is not the same as keeping wages up, as we have seen. Incomes move *down* as wages move up from the free market point."

Why Depressions Disrupt

"Wages are to a considerable extent under future contract. Even without a contract, wage reductions are resisted strongly, even though with lower prices, the lower wage would buy as much as before.

"A wage that is supported at its former level when other prices are declining is the same as a wage increase when other prices are remaining the same. And so in a depression like that of the thirties, supporting wages at their old level puts them above the free market level, just as if they had been pushed upward arbitrarily when prices were stable. The result is unemployment––three to one unemployment.

"Politicians and business executives also arrive on the stage at about this time to lend their 'help.' They also try to hold wages up. This is precisely the wrong thing to do. It merely makes matters worse, like doing something to maintain the blood pressure of a person with high blood pressure.

"All in all, 'help' at such times is dangerous. Controlling wages amounts to threatening the life of the patient, who would quickly recover as he always has done in the past when left to resolve his own problems––if he is free to continue to work at the best price a free market will offer him."

Harper then shows that profits and employment go together and thus disprove the Marxian theory. A chart of business instability from 1800 to 1955 shows that business was relatively stable from 1820 to 1929 and then exceedingly unstable. "Then came the Great Depression. Instability of business since 1929, and continuing even up to the present, is something unprecedented in our history. This instability of the last quarter century certainly cannot be called, correctly, a continuation of any long-time upward trend in business fluctuations under our increasing industrialization of the past century. It is something distinct and suddenly new in our economy––a degree of instability above anything we have ever before known in this country."

It is demonstrated that the increasing instability is caused by the increasing controls and that prosperity requires elimination of the controls which in the long run cause unemployment.

The final statement is that some minor business instability is essential to progress. "My own conclusion is that we should not worry about all such fluctuations in business at all. We should worry only about those fluctuations which are due to prohibitions on the right of each person to work at a job of his choice——either for himself or for an employer who wants his labor——at a wage mutually satisfactory between them. We should worry only about prohibitions on the spending of his income for what he wants most, among things offered by others who have produced them from their own labors.

"If we do this, business fluctuations will be reduced to whatever fluctuation people want. Wages would then be as high and would rise as rapidly as is possible. Leisure, to the extent one can afford it and wants it, would then be chosen as each person so desires. These conditions would give the maximum of welfare possible for us to attain at any time. It would be as near a utopia as can be hoped for in economic affairs this side of Heaven."

CHAPTER V

THE ECONOMIC BASIS
FOR PROSPERITY

The Harper essay covers its particular subject of "Why Wages Rise," but a much broader understanding is required to expose all of the insidious and deadly fallacies of socialism. The best short and simple book on this subject for the average citizen is *Economics in One Lesson* by Henry Hazlitt.[1] It ran through 15 printings in the hardcover edition, was the Executive Book Club selection, was condensed in *The Reader's Digest* and made a special reprint by *The Reader's Digest* and the Tax Foundation. Typical acclaim: "It is a brilliant performance. It says precisely the things which need most saying and says them with a rare courage and integrity. I know of no other modern book from which the intelligent layman can learn so much about the basic truths of economics in so short a time." F. A. Hayek, author of *The Road to Serfdom*.

This review and condensation is intended to show the scope and clarity of the book and whet the reader's appetite for a deeper understanding of the simple but fundamental principles of economics. *Economics in One Lesson* is a book which should be read, and reread,

---

[1] Henry Hazlitt is justly famous both as economic journalist and economic scholar. He had a regular column in *Newsweek* and his two critiques of Keynesian economics are classic.

until thoroughly understood by every intelligent citizen. Quotes and comments on each chapter follow.

PREFACE

"This book is an analysis of economic fallacies that are at last so prevalent that they have almost become a new orthodoxy. The one thing that has prevented this has been their own self-contradictions, which have scattered those who accept the same premises into a hundred different 'schools,' for the simple reason that it is impossible in matters touching practical life to be consistently wrong. But the difference between one new school and another is merely that one group wakes up earlier than another to the absurdities to which its false premises are driving it, and becomes at that moment inconsistent by either unwittingly abandoning its false premises or accepting conclusions from them less disturbing or fantastic than those logic would demand.

"There is not a major government in the world at this moment, however, whose economic policies are not influenced if they are not almost wholly determined by acceptance of some of these fallacies. Perhaps the shortest and surest way to an understanding of economics is through a dissection of such errors, and particularly of the central error from which they stem."

Hazlitt continues with a discussion of earlier writers and gives special credit to Frederic Bastiat, Philip Wicksteed and Ludwig von Mises.

1. THE LESSON

"Economics is haunted by more fallacies than any other study known to man. This is no accident. The inherent difficulties of the subject would be great enough in any case, but they are multiplied a thousand-fold by a factor that is insignificant in, say, physics, mathematics or medicine—— the special pleading of selfish interests. While every group has certain economic interests identical with those of all groups, every group has also, as we shall see, interests antagonistic to those of all other groups. While certain public policies would in the long run benefit everybody, other policies would benefit one group only at the expense of all other groups. The group that would benefit by such policies, having such a direct interest in them, will argue for them plausibly and persistently. It will hire the best buyable minds to devote their whole time to presenting its case. And it will finally either convince the general public that its case is sound, or so befuddle it that clear thinking on the subject becomes next to impossible.

"In addition to these endless pleadings of self-interest, there is a second main factor that spawns new economic fallacies every day. This is the persistent tendency of men to see only the immediate effects of a given policy, or its effect only on a special group, and to neglect to inquire what the long-run effects of that policy will be not only to that special group but on all groups. It is the fallacy of overlooking secondary consequences.

"In this lies almost the whole difference between good economics and bad. The bad economist sees only what immediately strikes the eye; the good economist also looks beyond. The bad economist sees only the direct consequences of a proposed course; the good economist looks also at the longer and indirect consequences. The bad economist sees only what the effect of a given policy has been or will be on one particular group; the good economist inquires also what the effect of the policy will be on all groups.

"*The art of economics consists in looking not merely at the immediate but at the longer effects of any act or policy; it consists in tracing the consequences of that policy not merely for one group but for all groups.*

"Nine-tenths of the economic fallacies that are working such dreadful harm in the world today are the result of ignoring this lesson. Those fallacies all stem from one of two central fallacies, or both; that of looking only at the immediate consequences of an act or proposal, and that of looking at the consequences only for a particular group to the neglect of other groups.

"It is often sadly remarked that the bad economists present their errors to the public better than the good economists present their truths. It is often complained that demagogues can be more plausible in putting forward economic nonsense from the platform than the honest men who try to show what is wrong with it. But the basic reason for this ought not to be mysterious. The reason is that the demagogues and bad economists are presenting half-truths. They are speaking only of the immediate effect of a proposed policy or its effect on a single group. As far as they go they may often be right. In these cases the answer consists in showing that the proposed policy would also have longer and less desirable effects, or that it could benefit one group only at the expense of all other groups. The answer consists in supplementing and correcting the half-truth with the other half. But to consider all the chief effects of a proposed course on everybody requires a long, complicated, and dull chain of reasoning. Most of the audience finds this chain of reasoning difficult to follow and soon becomes bored and inattentive. The bad economists rationalize this intellectual debility and laziness by assuring the audience that it need not even attempt to follow the reasoning or judge it on its merits because it is only 'classicism' or 'laissez faire' or 'capitalist apologetics' or whatever other term of abuse may happen to strike them as effective.

"We have stated the nature of the lesson, and of the fallacies that stand in its way, in abstract terms. But the lesson will not be driven home, and the fallacies will continue to go unrecognized, unless both are illustrated by examples. Through these examples we can move from the most elementary problems in economics to the most complex and difficult. Through them we can learn to detect and avoid first the crudest and most palpable fallacies and finally some of the most sophisticated and elusive. To that task we shall now proceed."

2. THE BROKEN WINDOW

"Let us begin with the simplest illustration possible: Let us, emulating Bastiat, choose a broken pane of glass.

"A young hoodlum, say, heaves a brick through the window of a baker's shop. The shopkeeper runs out furious, but the boy is gone. A crowd gathers, and begins to stare with quiet satisfaction at the gaping hole in the window and the shattered glass over the bread and pies. After a while the crowd feels the need for philosophic reflection. And several of its members are almost certain to remind each other or the baker that, after all, the misfortune has its bright side. It will make business for some glazier. As they begin to think of this they will elaborate upon it. How much does a new plate glass window cost? A hundred dollars? That will be quite a sum. After all, if windows were never broken, what would happen to the glass business? Then, of course, the thing is endless. The glazier will have $100 more to spend with other merchants, and these in turn will have $100 more to spend with still other merchants, and so on ad infinitum. The smashed window will go on providing money and employment in ever-widening circles. The logical conclusion from all this would be, if the crowd drew it, that the little hoodlum who threw the brick, far from being a public menace, was a public benefactor.

"Now let us take another look. The crowd is at least right in its first conclusion. This little act of vandalism will in the first instance mean more business for some glazier. The glazier will be no more unhappy to learn of the incident than an undertaker to learn of a death. But the shopkeeper will be out $100 that he was planning to spend for a new suit. Because he has had to replace a window, he will have to go without the suit (or some equivalent need or luxury). Instead of having a window and $100 he now has merely a window. Or, as he was planning to buy the suit that very afternoon, instead of having both a window and a suit he must be content with the window and no suit. If we think of him as a part of the community, the community has lost a new suit that otherwise might have come into being, and is just that much poorer.

"The glazier's gain of business, in short, is merely the tailor's loss of business. No new 'employment' has been added. The people in the crowd were thinking only of two parties to the transaction, the baker and glazier. They had forgotten the potential third party involved, the tailor. They forgot him precisely because he will not now enter the scene. They will see the new window in the next day or two. They will never see the extra suit, precisely because it will never be made. They see only what is immediately visible to the eye.

3. THE BLESSINGS OF DESTRUCTION

"So we have finished with the broken window. An elementary fallacy. Anybody, one would think, would be able to avoid it after a few moments' thought. Yet the broken window fallacy, under a hundred disguises, is the most persistent in the history of economics. It is more rampant now than at any time in the past. It is solemnly reaffirmed every day by great captains of industry, by chambers of commerce, by labor union leaders, by editorial writers and newspaper columnists and radio commentators, by learned statisticians using the most refined techniques, by professors of economics in our best universities. In their various ways they all dilate the advantages of destruction.

"Though some of them would disdain to say that there are net benefits in small acts of destruction, they see almost endless benefits in enormous acts of destruction. They tell us how much better off economically we all are in war than in peace. They see 'miracles of production' which it requires a war to achieve. And they see a world made prosperous by an enormous 'accumulated' or 'backed-up' demand. In Europe they joyously counted the houses, the whole cities that had been leveled to the ground and that 'had to be replaced.' In America they counted the houses that could not be built during the war, the nylon stockings that could not be supplied, the worn-out automobiles and tires, the obsolescent radios and refrigerators. They brought together formidable totals.

"It was merely our old friend, the broken-window fallacy, in new clothing, and grown beyond recognition. This time it was supported by a whole bundle of related fallacies. It confused *need* with *demand*. The more war destroys, the more it impoverishes, the greater is the post-war need. Indubitably. But need is not demand. Effective economic demand requires not merely need but corresponding purchasing power. The needs of India are incomparably greater than the needs in America. But its purchasing power, and therefore the new business that it can stimulate, are incomparably smaller.

"But if we get past this point, there is a chance for another fallacy, and the broken-windowites usually grab it. They think of 'purchasing power' merely in terms of money. Now money can be run off by the printing press. As this is being written, in fact, printing money is the world's biggest industry——if the product is measured in monetary terms. But the more money is turned out in this way, the more the value of any given unit of money falls. This falling value can be measured in rising prices of commodities. But as most people are so firmly in the habit of thinking of their wealth and income in terms of money, they consider themselves better off as these monetary totals rise, in spite of the fact that in terms of things they may have less and buy less.

"Now there is a half-truth in the 'backed-up' demand fallacy, just as there was in the broken-window fallacy. The broken window did make more business for the glazier. The destruction of war did make more business for the producers of certain things. The destruction of houses and cities did make more business for the building and construction industries. The inability to produce automobiles, radios, and refrigerators during the war did bring about a cumulative post-war demand *for those particular products.*

"To most people this seemed like an increase in total demand, as it partly was *in terms of dollars of lower purchasing power.* But what mainly took place was a diversion of demand to these particular products from others. The people of Europe built more new houses than otherwise because they had to. But when they built more houses they had just that much less manpower and productive capacity left over for everything else.

"Those who think that the destruction of war increases total 'demand' forget that demand and supply are merely two sides of the same coin. Supply increases demand because at bottom it *is* demand.

"This fundamental fact, it is true, is obscured for most people (including some reputedly brilliant economists) through such complications as wage payments and the indirect form in which virtually all modern exchanges are made through the medium of money. John Stuart Mill and other classical writers, . . . at least saw through 'the monetary veil' to the underlying realities. To that extent they were in advance of many of their present-day critics, who are befuddled by money rather than instructed by it. Mere inflation––that is, the mere issuance of more money, with the consequence of higher wages and prices––may *look* like the creation of more demand. But in terms of the actual production and exchange of real things it is not. It should be obvious that real buying power is wiped out to the same extent as productive power is wiped out.

"We are brought, in brief, to the conclusion that it is never an advantage to have one's plants destroyed by shells or bombs.

"In all this discussion, moreover, we have so far omitted a central consideration. Plants and equipment cannot be replaced by an individual (or a socialist government) unless he or it has acquired or can acquire the savings, the capital accumulation, to make the replacement. But war destroys accumulated capital. Postwar demand will never reproduce the precise pattern of prewar demand. But such complications should not divert us from recognizing the basic truth that the wanton destruction of anything of real value is always a net loss, a misfortune, or a disaster."

4. PUBLIC WORKS MEANS TAXES

"There is no more persistent and influential faith in the world today than the faith in government spending. Everywhere government spending is presented as a panacea for all our economic ills. Is private industry partially stagnant? We can fix it all by government spending. Is there unemployment? That is obviously due to 'insufficient private purchasing power.' The remedy is just as obvious. All that is necessary is for the government to spend enough to make up the 'deficiency.'

"An enormous literature is based on this fallacy, and, as so often happens with doctrines of this sort, it has become part of an intricate network of fallacies that mutually support each other. We cannot explore that whole network at this point; . . . but we can examine here the mother fallacy that has given birth to this progeny, the main stem of the network.

"Everything we get, outside of the free gifts of nature, must in some way be paid for.

"Having put aside for later consideration the network of fallacies which rest on chronic government borrowing and inflation, we shall take it for granted throughout the present chapter that either immediately or ultimately every dollar of government spending must be raised through a dollar of taxation. Once we look at the matter in this way, the supposed miracles of government spending will appear in another light.

"A certain amount of public spending is necessary to perform essential government functions. A certain amount of public works—— of streets and roads and bridges and tunnels, of armories and navy yards, of buildings to house legislatures, police and fire departments——is necessary to supply essential public services. With such public works, necessary for their own sake, and defended on that ground alone, I am not here concerned. I am here concerned with public works considered as a means of 'providing employment' or of adding wealth to the community that it would not otherwise have had."

Hazlitt then discusses the building of a bridge which was not really necessary and shows that its cost diverted an equal purchasing power from the taxpayers.

"The same reasoning applies, of course, to every other form of public work. It applies just as well, for example, to the erection, with public funds, of housing for people of low incomes. All that happens is that money is taken away through taxes from families of higher income (and perhaps a little from families of even lower income) to force them to subsidize these selected families with low incomes and enable them to live in better housing for the same rent or for lower rent than previously.

"I do not intend to enter here into all the pros and cons of public housing. I am concerned only to point out the error in two of the arguments most frequently put forward in favor of public housing. One is the argument that it 'creates employment'; the other is that it creates wealth which would not otherwise have been produced. Both of these arguments are false, because they overlook what is lost through taxation. Taxation for public housing destroys as many jobs in other lines as it creates in housing. It also results in unbuilt private homes, in unmade washing machines and refrigerators, and in lack of innumerable other commodities and services.

"The great psychological advantage of the public housing advocates is that men are seen at work on the houses when they are going up, and the houses are seen when they are finished. People live in them, and proudly show their friends through the rooms. The jobs destroyed by the taxes for the housing are not seen, nor are the goods and services that were never made. It takes a concentrated effort of thought, and a new effort each time the houses and happy people in them are seen, to think of the wealth that was not created instead.

"We must apply the same reasoning, once more, to great projects like the Tennessee Valley Authority. Here, because of sheer size, the danger of optical illusion is greater than ever. Here is a mighty dam, a stupendous arc of steel and concrete, 'greater than anything that private capital could have built,' the fetish of photographers, the heaven of socialists, the most often used symbol of the miracles of public construction, ownership and operation. Here are mighty generators and power houses. Here is a whole region, it is said, lifted to a higher economic level, attracting factories and industries that could not otherwise have existed. And it is all presented, in the panegyrics of its partisans, as a net economic gain without offsets.

"We need not go here into the merits of the TVA[2] or public projects like it. But this time we need a special effort of the imagination, which few people seem able to make, to look at the debit side of the ledger. If taxes are taken from people and corporations, and spent in one particular section of the country, why should it cause surprise, why should it be regarded as a miracle, if that section becomes relatively richer? Other sections of the country, we should remember, are then comparatively poorer. The thing so great that 'private capital could not have built it' has in fact been built by private capital—the capital that was expropriated in taxes (or, if the money was borrowed, that eventually must be expropriated in taxes).

"I have deliberately chosen the most favorable examples of public spending schemes—that is, those that are most frequently and fervently

---

[2] For an excellent discussion of the merits of TVA read "The TVA Idea" by Dean Russell, published by FEE .

urged by the government spenders and most highly regarded by the public. I have not spoken of the hundreds of boondoggling projects that are invariably embarked upon the moment the main object is to 'give jobs' and 'to put people to work.' For then the usefulness of the project itself, as we have seen, inevitably becomes a subordinate consideration. Moreover, the more wasteful the work, the more costly in manpower, the better it becomes for the purpose of providing more employment. Under such circumstances it is highly improbable that the projects thought up by the bureaucrats will provide the same net addition to wealth and welfare, per dollar expended, as would have been provided by the taxpayers themselves, if they had been individually permitted to buy or have made what they themselves wanted, instead of being forced to surrender part of their earnings to the state."

5. TAXES DISCOURAGE PRODUCTION

This subject is so basic and the chapter so concise that it is quoted in full except for the short introduction.

"In our modern world there is never the same percentage of income tax levied on everybody. The great burden of income taxes is imposed on a minor percentage of the nation's income; and these income taxes have to be supplemented by taxes of other kinds. These taxes inevitably affect the actions and incentives of those from whom they are taken. When a corporation loses a hundred cents of every dollar it loses, and is permitted to keep only 48 cents of every dollar it gains, and when it cannot offset its years of losses against its years of gains, or cannot do so adequately, its policies are affected. It does not expand its operations, or it expands only those attended with a minimum of risk. People who recognize this situation are deterred from starting new enterprises. Thus old employers do not give more employment, or not as much as they might have; and others decide not to become employers at all. Improved machinery and better equipped factories come into existence much more slowly than they otherwise would. The result in the long run is that consumers are prevented from getting better and cheaper products to the extent that they otherwise would, and that real wages are held down, compared with what they might have been.

"There is a similar effect when personal incomes are taxed 50, 60, 75 and 90 per cent. People begin to ask themselves why they should work six, eight or ten months of the entire year for the government, and only six, four or two months for themselves and their families. If they lose the whole dollar when they lose, but can keep only a fraction of it when they win, they decide that it is foolish to take risks with their capital. In addition, the capital available for risk-taking itself shrinks enormously. It is being taxed away before it can be accumulated. In brief, capital to provide new private jobs is first prevented from coming into existence, and the part that does come into existence is then discouraged from starting new enterprises. The government spenders create the very problem of unemployment that they profess to solve.

"A certain amount of taxes is of course indispensable to carry on essential government functions. Reasonable taxes for this purpose need not hurt production much. The kind of government services then supplied in return, which among other things safeguard production itself, more than compensate for this. But the larger the percentage of the national income taken by taxes the greater the deterrent to private production and employment. When the total tax burden grows beyond a bearable size, the problem of devising taxes that will not discourage and disrupt production becomes insoluble."

6. CREDIT DIVERTS PRODUCTION

"Government 'encouragement' to business is sometimes as much to be feared as government hostility. This supposed encouragement often takes the form of a direct grant of government credit or a guarantee of private loans."

Hazlitt clearly shows that government lending, or guaranteed loans, inherently has higher risk than private loans and that this actually means placing scarce capital equipment in the hands of less qualified operators. He first discusses farm loans and then continues: "The case becomes even clearer if we turn from farming to other forms of business. The proposal is frequently made that the government ought to assume the risks that are 'too great for private industry.' This means that bureaucrats should be permitted to take risks with the taxpayer's money that no one is willing to take with his own.

"Such a policy would lead to evils of many different kinds. It would lead to favoritism; to the making of loans to friends, or in return for bribes. It would inevitably lead to scandals. It would lead to recriminations whenever the taxpayer's money was thrown away on enterprises that failed. It would increase the demand for socialism; for, it would properly be asked, if the government is going to bear the risks, why should it not also get the profits? What justification could there possibly be, in fact, for asking the taxpayers to take the risks while permitting private capitalists to keep the profits? (This is precisely, however, as we shall later see, what we already do in the case of 'non-recourse' government loans to farmers).

"But we shall pass over all these evils for the moment, and concentrate on just one consequence of loans of this type. This is that they will waste capital and reduce production. They will throw the available capital into bad or at best dubious projects. They will throw it into the hands of persons who are less competent or less trustworthy than those who would otherwise have got it. For the amount of real capital at any moment (as distinguished from monetary tokens run off on a printing press) is limited. What is put into the hands of B cannot be put into the hands of A.

"The private lenders, moreover, are selected by a cruel market test. If they make bad mistakes they lose their money and have no more money to lend. It is only if they have been successful in the past that they have more money to lend in the future. Thus private lenders (except the relatively small proportion that have got their funds through inheritance) are rigidly selected by a process of survival of the fittest. The government lenders, on the other hand, are either those who have passed civil service examinations, and know how to answer hypothetical questions hypothetically, or they are those who can give the most plausible reasons for making loans and the most plausible explanations of why it wasn't their fault that the loans failed. But the net result remains: private loans will utilize existing resources and capital far better than government loans. Government loans will waste far more capital and resources than private loans. Government loans, in short, as compared with private loans, will reduce production, not increase it.

"The proposal for government loans to private individuals or projects, in brief, sees B and forgets A. It sees the people into whose hands the capital is put; it forgets those who would otherwise have had it. It sees the project to which capital is granted; it forgets the projects from which capital is thereby withheld. It sees the immediate benefit to one group; it overlooks the losses to other groups, and the net loss to the community as a whole."

7. THE CURSE OF MACHINERY

"Among the most viable of all economic delusions is the belief that machines on net balance create unemployment. This fallacy is still the basis of many labor union practices. The public tolerates these practices because it either believes at bottom that the unions are right, or is too confused to see just why they are wrong. The belief that machines cause unemployment, when held with any logical consistency, leads to preposterous conclusions."

Hazlitt gives a few facts from the early days of the industrial revolution and tells of the actual pitched battles and the destruction of thousands of machines by workers who feared loss of jobs. Some jobs were lost temporarily but in the 27 years after the invention of the cotton spinning machinery, cotton cloth workers increased from 7,900 to 320,000, an increase of 4400%.

"One might pile up mountains of figures to show how wrong were the technophobes of the past. But it would do no good unless we understand clearly *why* they were wrong. For statistics and history are useless in economics unless accompanied by a basic *deductive* understanding of the facts—which means in this case an understanding of why the past consequences of the introduction of machinery and other labor-saving devices *had* to occur." Particular cases are then discussed which show that: "In brief, on net balance, machines, technological improvements, automation, economics and efficiency do not throw men out of work."

Other types of invention involve new or improved materials or new services but in each case the overall result is not a loss of jobs. "There is also an absolute sense in which machines may be said to have enormously increased the number of jobs. The population of the world today is three times as great as in the middle of the eighteenth century, before the Industrial Revolution had got well under way. Machines may be said to have given birth to this increased population; for without the machines, the world would not have been able to support it. Two out of every three of us, therefore, may be said to owe not only our jobs but our very lives to machines.

"Yet it is a misconception to think of the function or result of machines as primarily one of creating *jobs*. The real result of the machine is to increase *production*, to raise the standard of living, to increase economic welfare. It is no trick to employ everybody, even (or especially) in the most primitive economy. Full employment—very full employment; long, weary, back-breaking employment—is characteristic of precisely the nations that are most retarded industrially. Where full employment already exists, new machines, inventions and discoveries cannot—until there has been time for an increase in the population—bring *more* employment. They are likely to bring more *un*employment (but this time I am speaking of *voluntary* and not involuntary *un*employment) because people can now afford to work fewer hours, while children and the over-aged no longer need to work.

"What machines do, to repeat, is to bring an increase in production and an increase in the standard of living. They may do this in either of two ways. They do it by making goods cheaper for consumers or they do it by increasing wages because they increase the productivity of the workers. In other words, they either increase money wages or, by reducing prices, they increase the goods and services that the same money wages will buy. Sometimes they do both. What actually happens will depend in large part upon the monetary policy pursued in a country. But in any case, machines, inventions and discoveries increase *real* wages."

8. SPREAD THE WORK SCHEMES

"I have referred to various union make-work and featherbed practices. The practices, and the public toleration of them, spring from the same fundamental fallacy as the fear of machines. This is the belief that a more efficient way of doing a thing destroys jobs, and the necessary corollary that a less efficient way of doing it creates them.

"Allied to this fallacy is the belief that there is just a fixed amount of work to be done in the world, and that, if we cannot add to this work by thinking up more cumbersome ways of doing it, at least we can think of devices for spreading it around among as large a number of people as possible.

"This error lies behind the minute subdivision of labor upon which unions insist. It is true that a few persons can profit at the expense of the rest of us from this arbitrary subdivision of labor——provided it happens in their case alone. But those who support it as a general practice fail to see that it always raises production costs; that it results on net balance in less work done and in fewer goods produced. The householder who is forced to employ two men to do the work of one has, it is true, given employment to one extra man. But he has just that much less money left over to spend on something that would employ somebody else. Because his bathroom leak has been repaired at double what it should have cost, he decides not to buy the new sweater he wanted. 'Labor' is no better off, because a day's employment of an unneeded tile-setter has meant a day's *dis*employment of a sweater knitter or machine handler. The householder, however, is worse off. Instead of having a repaired shower and a sweater, he has the shower and no sweater. And if we count the sweater as part of the national wealth, the country is short one sweater. This symbolizes the net result of the effort to make extra work by arbitrary subdivision of labor.

"But there are other schemes for 'spreading the work,' often put forward by union spokesmen and legislators. The most frequent of these is the proposal to shorten the work week, usually by law. The belief that it would 'spread the work' and 'give more jobs' was one of the main reasons behind the inclusion of the penalty-overtime provision in the existing Federal Wage-Hour Law."

Hazlitt then discusses the two possibilities: a) decrease in hours at a constant wage rate and, b) increasing the rate to maintain a constant total wage. He shows that total production is reduced either way and that workers in general are worse off. He concludes: "The spread-the-work schemes, in brief, rest on the same sort of illusion that we have been considering. The people who support such schemes think only of the employment they would provide for particular persons or groups; they do not stop to consider what their whole effect would be on everybody.

"The spread-the-work schemes rest also, as we began by pointing out, on the false assumption that there is just a fixed amount of work to be done. There could be no greater fallacy. There is no limit to the amount of work to be done as long as any human need or wish that work could fill remains unsatisfied. In a modern exchange economy, the most work will be done when prices, costs and wages are in the best relations with each other. What these relations are we shall later consider."

9. DISBANDING TROOPS AND BUREAUCRATS

"When, after every great war, it is proposed to demobilize the armed forces, there is always a great fear that there will not be enough jobs for these forces and that in consequence they will be unemployed. It is true that, when millions of men are suddenly released, it may require time for private industry to reabsorb them——though what has been chiefly remarkable in the past has been the speed, rather than the slowness, with which this was accomplished. The fears of unemployment arise because people look at only one side of the process.

"They see soldiers being turned loose on the labor market. Where is the 'purchasing power' going to come from to employ them? If we assume that the public budget is being balanced, the answer is simple. The government will cease to support the soldiers. But the taxpayers will be allowed to retain the funds that were previously taken from them in order to support the soldiers. And the taxpayers will then have additional funds to buy additional goods. Civilian demand, in other words, will be increased, and will give employment to the added labor force represented by the soldiers.

"But the demobilization will not leave us economically just where we were before it started. The soldiers previously supported by civilians will not become merely civilians supported by other civilians. They will become self-supporting civilians. If we assume that the men who would otherwise have been retained in the armed services are no longer needed for defense, then their retention would have been sheer waste. They would have been unproductive. The taxpayers, in return for supporting them, would have got nothing. But now the taxpayers turn over this part of their funds to them as fellow civilians in return for equivalent goods or services. Total national production, the wealth of everybody, is higher.

"The same reasoning applies to civilian government officials whenever they are retained in excessive numbers and do not perform services for their community reasonably equivalent to the remuneration they receive.

"Once again the fallacy comes from looking at the effects of this action only on the dismissed officeholders themselves and on the particular tradesmen who depend upon them. Once again it is forgotten that, if these bureaucrats are not retained in office, the taxpayers will be permitted to keep the money that was formerly taken from them for the support of the bureaucrats. Once again it is forgotten that the taxpayers' income and purchasing power go up by at least as much as the income and purchasing power of the former officeholders go down. If the particular shopkeepers who formerly got the business of these bureaucrats lose trade other shopkeepers elsewhere gain at least as much. Washington is less prosperous, and can, perhaps, support fewer stores but other towns can support more.

"Once again, however, the matter does not end there. The country is not merely as well off without the superfluous officeholders as it would have been had it retained them. It is much better off. For the officeholders must now seek private jobs or set up private businesses.

And the added purchasing power of the taxpayers, as we have noted in the case of the soldiers, will encourage this. But the officeholders can take private jobs only by supplying equivalent services to those who provide the jobs––or, rather, to the customers of the employers who provide the jobs. Instead of being parasites, they become productive men and women.

"This 'purchasing power' argument is, when one considers it seriously, fantastic. It could just as well apply to a racketeer or a thief who robs you. After he takes your money he has more purchasing power. He supports with it bars, restaurants, night clubs, tailors, perhaps automobile workers. But for every job his spending provides, your own spending must provide one less, because you have that much less to spend. Just so the taxpayers provide one less job for every job supplied by the spending of officeholders. When your money is taken by a thief, you get nothing in return. When your money is taken through taxes to support needless bureaucrats, precisely the same situation exists. We are lucky, indeed, if the needless bureaucrats are merely easygoing loafers. They are more likely today to be energetic reformers busily discouraging and disrupting production."

10. THE FETISH OF FULL EMPLOYMENT

"The economic goal of any nation, as of any individual, is to get the greatest results with the least effort. The whole economic progress of mankind has consisted in getting more production with the same labor. It is for this reason that men began putting burdens on the backs of mules instead of their own; that they went on to invent the wheel and the wagon, the railroad and the motor truck. It is for this reason that men used their ingenuity to develop a hundred thousand labor-saving inventions.

"All this is so elementary that one would blush to state it if it were not being constantly forgotten by those who coin and circulate new slogans. Translated into national terms, this first principle means that our real objective is to maximize production. In doing this, full employment––that is, the absence of involuntary idleness––becomes a necessary by-product. But production is the end, employment merely the means. We cannot continuously have the fullest production without full employment. But we can very easily have full employment without full production. The slave labor in Germany had full employment. Prisons and chain-gangs have full employment. Coercion always provides full employment.

"The progress of civilization has meant the reduction of employment, not its increase. It is because we have become increasingly wealthy as a nation that we have been able virtually to eliminate child labor, to remove the necessity of work for many of the aged and to make it unnecessary for millions of women to take jobs. A much smaller proportion of the American population needs to work than that, say, of China or Russia. The real question is not how many millions of jobs there will be in America ten years from now, but how much shall we produce, and what, in consequence, will be our standard of living? The problem of distribution, on which all the stress is being put today, is after all more easily solved the more there is to distribute.

"We can clarify our thinking if we put our chief emphasis where it belongs––on policies that will maximize production."

11. WHO'S "PROTECTED" BY TARIFFS?

"A mere recital of the economic policies of government all over the world is calculated to cause any serious student of economics to throw up his hands in despair. What possible point can there be, he is likely to ask, in discussing refinements and advances in economic theory, when popular thought and the actual policies of governments, certainly in everything connected with international relations, have not yet caught up with Adam Smith? For present day tariff and trade policies are not only as bad as those in the seventeenth and eighteenth centuries, but incomparably worse.

"Since *The Wealth of Nations* appeared nearly two centuries ago, the case for free trade has been stated thousands of times, but perhaps never with more direct simplicity and force than it was stated in that volume. In general, Smith rested his case on one fundamental proposition: 'In every country it always is and must be the interest of the great body of the people to buy whatever they want of those who sell it cheapest.' 'The proposition is so very manifest,' Smith continued, 'that it seems ridiculous to take any pains to prove it; nor could it ever have been called in question, had not the interested sophistry of merchants and manufacturers confounded the common-sense of mankind.'

"From another point of view, free trade was considered as one aspect of the specialization of labor:

> 'It is the maxim of every prudent master of a family, never to attempt to make at home what it will cost him more to make than to buy. The tailor does not attempt to make his own shoes, but buys them of the shoemaker. The shoemaker does not attempt to make his own clothes, but employs a tailor. The farmer attempts to make neither the one nor the other, but employs those different artificers. All of them find it to their interest to employ their whole industry in a way in which they have some advantage over their neighbors, and to purchase with a part of its produce, or what is the same thing, with the price of a part of it, whatever else they have occasion for. What is prudence in the conduct of every private family can scarce be folly in that of a great kingdom.'

"But whatever led people to suppose that what was prudence in the conduct of every private family *could* be folly in that of a great kingdom? It was a whole network of fallacies, out of which mankind has still been unable to cut its way. And the chief of them was the central fallacy with which this book is concerned. It was that of considering merely the immediate effects of a tariff on special groups, and neglecting to consider its long-run effects on the whole community."

After this introduction, Hazlitt gives examples of tariff protection to build or protect industry and he shows that: "The effect of a tariff, therefore, is to change the *structure* of American production. It changes the number of occupations, the kind of occupations, and the relative size of one industry as compared with another. It makes the industries in which we are comparatively inefficient larger, and the industries in which we are comparatively efficient smaller. Its net effect, therefore, is to reduce American efficiency, as well as to reduce efficiency in the countries with which we would otherwise have traded more largely. But a tariff is not irrelevant to the question of wages. In the long run it always reduces real wages, because it reduces efficiency, production and wealth."

This concludes with the reminder that a tariff: "does benefit––or at least *can* benefit *special interests*. True it benefits them *at the expense of everyone else*."

12. THE DRIVE FOR EXPORTS

"Exceeded only by the pathological dread of imports that affects all nations is a pathological yearning for exports. Logically, it is true, nothing could be more inconsistent. It is exports that pay for imports, and vice versa. The greater exports we have, the greater imports we must have, if we ever expect to get paid."

Hazlitt briefly discusses foreign trade and loans, concluding: "Now the same people who can be clearheaded and sensible when the subject is one of domestic trade can be incredibly emotional and muddleheaded when it becomes one of foreign trade. In the latter field they can seriously advocate or acquiesce in principles which they would think it insane to apply in domestic business. A typical example is the belief that the government should make huge loans to foreign countries for the sake of increasing our exports, regardless of whether or not these loans are likely to be repaid.

"It should be immediately obvious that if the loans we make to foreign countries to enable them to buy our goods are not repaid, then we are giving our goods away. Here we have simply one more example of the error of looking only at the immediate effect of a policy on some special group, and of not having the patience or intelligence to trace the long-run effects of the policy on everyone.

"If we do trace these long-run effects on everyone, we come to an additional conclusion––the exact opposite of the doctrine that has dominated the thinking of most government officials for centuries. This is, as John Stuart Mill so clearly pointed out, that the real gain of foreign trade to any country lies not in its exports but in its imports. Its consumers are either able to get from abroad commodities at a lower price than they could obtain them for at home, or commodities that they could not get from domestic producers at all. Collectively considered, the real reason a country needs exports is to pay for its imports."

13. 'PARITY' PRICES

"Special interests, as the history of tariffs reminds us, can think of the most ingenious reasons why they should be the objects of special solicitude. Their spokesmen present a plan in their favor; and it seems at first so absurd that disinterested writers do not trouble to expose it. But the special interests keep on insisting on the scheme. Its enactment would make so much difference to their own immediate welfare that they can afford to hire trained economists and 'public relations experts' to propagate it in their behalf. The public hears the argument so often repeated, and accompanied by such a wealth of imposing statistics, charts, curves and pie-slices, that it is soon taken in. When at last disinterested writers recognize that the danger of the scheme's enactment is real, they are usually too late. They cannot in a few weeks acquaint themselves with the subject as thoroughly as the hired brains who have been devoting their full time to it for years; they are accused of being uninformed, and they have the air of men who presume to dispute axioms."

This introduction could apply equally well to almost any phase of economics. Hazlitt gives a brief history of 'parity prices' and then discusses 'compensating' farmers for tariffs on the manufactured goods which they purchase. "If a city worker has to pay a higher price for woolen blankets or overcoats because of a tariff, is he 'compensated' by having to pay a higher price also for cotton clothing and for foodstuffs? Or is he merely being robbed twice? So the alleged benefits of still another scheme evaporate as soon as we trace not only its immediate effects on a special group but its long-run effects on everyone."

14. SAVING THE "X" INDUSTRY

Hazlitt discusses various declining industries and governmental efforts to preserve them. He concludes that if an industry is dying a natural death: "Why should it be kept alive by artificial respiration? The idea that an expanding economy implies that *all* industries must be simultaneously expanding is a profound error. In order that new industries may grow fast enough it is usually necessary that some old industries should be allowed to shrink or die. In doing this they help to release the necessary capital and labor for the new industries. If we had tried to keep the horse-and-buggy trade artificially alive we would have slowed down the growth of the automobile industry and all the trades dependent on it. We would have lowered the production of wealth and retarded economic and scientific progress.

"We do the same thing, however, when we try to prevent any industry from dying in order to protect the labor already trained or the capital already invested in it. Paradoxical as it may seem to some, it is just as necessary to the health of a dynamic economy that dying industries be allowed to die as that growing industries be allowed to grow. The first process is essential to the second. It is as foolish to try to preserve obsolescent industries as to try to preserve obsolescent methods of production; this is often, in fact, merely two ways of describing the same thing. Improved methods of production must constantly supplant obsolete methods, if both old needs and new wants are to be filled by better commodities and better means."

15. HOW THE PRICE SYSTEM WORKS

"The whole argument of this book may be summed up in the statement that in studying the effects of any given economic proposal we must trace not merely the immediate results but the results in the long run, not merely the primary consequences but the secondary consequences, and not merely the effects on some special group but the effects on everyone. It follows that it is foolish and misleading to concentrate our attention merely on some special point––to examine, for example, merely what happens in one industry without considering what happens in all. But it is precisely from the persistent and lazy habit of thinking only of some particular industry or process in isolation that the major fallacies of economics stem. These fallacies pervade not merely the arguments of the hired spokesmen of special interests, but the arguments even of some economists who pass as profound."

Hazlitt outlines briefly the basic problems of a Robinson Crusoe and the slightly more complicated "alternative applications of time and labor" for a Swiss Family Robinson. He then shows that even a highly complex society has the same fundamental choices and that freely changing prices guide all elements of a free society to make the best possible choices.

"It is only the much vilified price system that solves the enormously complicated problem of deciding precisely how much of tens of thousands of different commodities and services should be produced in relation to each other. These otherwise bewildering equations are solved quasi-automatically by the system of prices, profits and costs. They are solved by this system incomparably better than any group of bureaucrats could solve them. For they are solved by a system under which each consumer makes his own demand and casts a fresh vote, or a dozen fresh votes, every day; whereas bureaucrats would try to solve it by having made for the consumers, not what the consumers themselves wanted, but what the bureaucrats decided was good for them.

"Yet though the bureaucrats do not understand the quasi-automatic system of the market, they are always disturbed by it. They are always trying to improve it or correct it, usually in the interests of some wailing pressure group."

16. 'STABILIZING' COMMODITIES

Under this subject are shown various simple and some complicated methods of raising prices; all of which distort the market and thus reduce over-all wellbeing. He concludes with international planning, as follows: "But if the planners succeed in tying up the idea of international co-operation with the increased State domination and control over economic life, the international controls of the future seem only too likely to follow the pattern of the past, in which case the plain man's living standards will decline with his liberties."

17. GOVERNMENT PRICE-FIXING

Prices set below normal must cause a shortage since consumption tends to increase and production decrease. The shortage then brings a demand for rationing and cost controls, until: "The natural consequence of a thorough-going over-all price control which seeks to perpetuate a given historic price level, in brief, must ultimately be a completely regimented economy. Wages would have to be held down as rigidly as prices. Labor would have to be rationed as ruthlessly as raw materials. The end result would be that the government would not only tell each consumer precisely how much of each commodity he could have, it would tell each manufacturer precisely what quantity of each raw material he could have and what quantity of labor. Competitive bidding for workers could no more be tolerated than competitive bidding for materials. The result would be a petrified totalitarian economy, with every business firm and every worker at the mercy of the government, and with final abandonment of all the traditional liberties we have known."

There also is a moral effect since controls bring on a 'Black Market' which gradually supplements legitimate trade channels. "During the transition period the large, long-established firms, with a heavy capital investment and a great dependence upon the retention of public good-will, are forced to restrict or discontinue production. Their place is taken by fly-by-night concerns with little capital and little accumulated experience in production. These new firms are inefficient compared with those they displace; they turn out inferior and dishonest goods at much higher production costs than the older concerns would have required for continuing to turn out their former goods. A premium is put on dishonesty. The new firms owe their very existence or growth to the fact that they are willing to violate the law; their customers conspire with them; and as a natural consequence demoralization spreads into all business practices.

"What lies at the base of the whole effort to fix maximum prices? There is first of all a misunderstanding of what it is that has been causing prices to rise. The real cause is either a scarcity of goods or a surplus of money. Legal price ceilings cannot cure either. In fact, as we have just seen, they merely intensify the shortage of goods. What to do about the surplus of money will be discussed in a later chapter. But one of the errors that lie behind the drive for price-fixing is the chief subject of this book. Just as the endless plans for raising prices of favored commodities are the result of thinking of the interests only of the producers immediately concerned, and forgetting the interests of consumers, so the plans for holding down prices by legal edict are the result of thinking of the short-run interests of people only as consumers and forgetting their interests as producers."

18. WHAT RENT CONTROL DOES

"Government control of the rents of houses and apartments is a special form of price control. Its consequences are substantially the same as those of government price control in general.

"When these consequences are so clear that they become glaring, there is of course no acknowledgement on the part of the advocates of rent control and the welfare statists that they have blundered. Instead, they denounce the capitalist system. They contend that private enterprise has 'failed again' that 'private enterprise cannot do the job.' Therefore, they will argue, the State must step in and itself build low-rent housing.

"This has been the almost universal result in every country that was involved in World War II or imposed rent control in an effort to offset monetary inflation.

"So the government launches on a gigantic housing program––at the taxpayers' expense. The houses are rented at a rate that does not pay back costs of construction or operation. A typical arrangement is for the government to pay annual subsidies, either directly to the tenants or to the builders or managers of the state housing. Whatever the nominal arrangement, the tenants in these buildings are being subsidized by the rest of the population. They are having part of their rent paid for them. They are being selected for favored treatment. The political possibilities of this favoritism are too clear to need stressing. A pressure group is built up which believes that the taxpayers owe it these subsidies as a matter of right. Another all but irreversible step is taken toward the total Welfare State.

"A final irony of rent control is that the more unrealistic, Draconian, and unjust it is, the more fervid the political arguments for its continuance.

"The pressure for rent control, in brief, comes from those who consider only its supposed short-run benefits to one group in the population. When we consider its effects on *all* groups, and especially when we consider its effect *in the long-run*, we recognize that rent control is not only increasingly futile, but increasingly harmful the more severe it is, and the longer it remains in effect."

19. MINIMUM WAGE LAWS

Wages are a price and it is shown that similar harmful results must follow any forced changes. Raising a worker's wage above his earning capacity means that he cannot be employed and thus he will starve if not given some relief. The required relief program complicates the problem by making it almost as profitable to "go on relief" as to work and this opens a whole new region for graft and corruption.[3]

"All this is not to argue that there is no way of raising wages. It is merely to point out that the apparently easy method of raising them by government fiat is the wrong way and the worst way.

---

[3] *Paying Men Not to Work*, FEE.

"This is perhaps as good a place as any to point out that what distinguishes many reformers from those who cannot accept their proposals is not their greater philanthropy, but their greater impatience. The question is not whether we wish to see everybody as well off as possible. Among men of good will such an aim can be taken for granted. The real question concerns the proper means of achieving it. And in trying to answer this we must never lose sight of a few elementary truisms. We cannot distribute more wealth than is created. We cannot in the long run pay labor as a whole more than it produces.

"The best way to raise wages, therefore, is to raise labor productivity. This can be done by many methods: by an increase in capital accumulation––i.e., by an increase in the machines with which the workers are aided; by new inventions and improvements; by more efficient management on the part of employers; by more industriousness and efficiency on the part of the workers; by better education and training. The more the individual worker produces, the more he increases the wealth of the whole community. The more he produces, the more his services are worth to employers, the more he will be paid. Real wages come out of production, not out of government decrees."

20. DO UNIONS REALLY RAISE WAGES?

"The belief that labor unions can substantially raise real wages over the long run and for the whole working population is one of the great delusions of the present age. This delusion is mainly the result of failure to recognize that wages are basically determined by labor productivity. It is for this reason, for example, that wages in the United States were incomparably higher than wages in England and Germany all during the decades when the 'labor movement' in the latter two countries was far more advanced."

Hazlitt discusses the real value of a union in assisting workers to obtain their proper (free-market) wage. "But it is easy, as experience has proved, for unions, particularly with the help of one-sided labor legislation which puts compulsion solely on employers, to go beyond their legitimate functions, to act irresponsibly, and to embrace short-sighted and anti-social policies. They do this, for example, whenever they seek to fix the wages of their members above their real market worth. Such an attempt always brings about unemployment. The arrangement can be made to stick, in fact, only by some form of intimidation or coercion.

"But the moment workers have to use intimidation or violence to enforce their demands—the moment they use mass-picketing to prevent any of the old workers from continuing at their jobs, or prevent the employers from hiring new permanent workers to take their places— their case becomes suspect. For the pickets are really being used, not primarily against the employer, but against other workers. These other workers are willing to take the jobs that the old employees have vacated, and at the wages that the old employees now reject.

"Emotional economics has given birth to theories that calm examination cannot justify. One of these is the idea that labor is being 'underpaid' *generally*. This would be analogous to the notion that in a free market prices in general are chronically too low. Another curious but persistent notion is that the interests of a nation's workers are identical with each other, and that an increase in wages for one union in some obscure way helps all other workers. Not only is there no truth in this idea; the truth is that, if a particular union by coercion is able to enforce for its own members a wage substantially above the real market worth of their services, it will hurt all other workers as it hurts other members of the community.

"When strong labor unions in the past made it their function to provide for their own unemployed members, they thought twice before demanding a wage that would cause heavy unemployment. But where there is a relief system under which the general taxpayer is forced to provide for the unemployment caused by excessive wage rates, this restraint on excessive union demands is removed."

Examples are given which show that excessive wage rates reduce production and cause unemployment. "Thus we are driven to the conclusion that unions, though they may for a time be able to secure an increase in money wages for their members, partly at the expense of employers and more at the expense of non-unionized workers, *cannot, in the long-run and for the whole body of workers, increase real wages at all.*

"One may go further than this conclusion, and raise the question whether unions have not, in the long run and for the whole body of workers, actually prevented real wages from rising to the extent to which they otherwise might have risen. They have certainly been a force working to hold down or reduce wages if their effect, on net balance, has been to reduce labor productivity; and we may ask whether it has not been so."

Various slowdown and make-work practices are analyzed and it is concluded:

> "Most of these policies have been followed under the assumption that there is just a fixed amount of work to be done, a definite 'job fund' which has to be spread over as many people and hours as possible so as not to use it up too soon. This assumption is utterly false. There is actually no limit to the amount of work to be done. Work creates work. What A produces constitutes the demand for what B produces.

"But because this false assumption exists, and because the policies of unions are based on it, their net effect has been to reduce productivity below what it would otherwise have been. Their net effect, therefore, in the long run and for all groups of workers, has been to *reduce* real wages––that is, wages in terms of the goods they will buy––below the level to which they would otherwise have risen. The real cause for the tremendous increase in real wages in the last half century (especially in America) has been, to repeat, the accumulation of capital and the enormous technological advance made possible by it.

"Reduction of the rate of increase in real wages is not, of course, a consequence inherent in the nature of unions. It has been the result of shortsighted policies."

21. "ENOUGH TO BUY BACK THE PRODUCT"

Hazlett discusses 'just' prices and wages as demanded by the Marxists and amateur economists. He outlines the lever effect as elaborated on by Paul Douglas (see page 83), that a change of one percent in wage rate causes a three percent change in employment and he concludes: "The best prices are not the highest prices, but the prices that encourage the largest volume of production and the largest volume of sales. The best wage rates for labor are not the highest wage rates, but the wage rates that permit full production, full employment and the largest sustained payrolls. The best profits, from the standpoint not only of industry but of labor, are not the lowest profits, but the profits that encourage most people to become employers or to provide more employment than before.

"If we try to run the economy for the benefit of a single group or class, we shall injure or destroy all groups, including the members of the very class for whose benefit we have been trying to run it. We must run the economy for everybody."

22. THE FUNCTION OF PROFIT

"The indignation shown by many people today at the mention of the very word 'profits' indicates how little understanding there is of the vital function that profits play in our economy.

"Profits actually do not bulk large in our total economy. Yet 'profits' are the form of income toward which there is most hostility.

"When the economy is free, demand so acts that some branches of production make what some government officials regard as 'excessive' or 'unreasonable' profits. But that very fact not only causes every firm in that line to expand its production to the utmost, and to reinvest its profits in more machinery and more employment; it also attracts new investors and producers from everywhere, until production in that line is great enough to meet demand, and the profits in it again fall to the general average level.

"In a free economy, in which wages, costs and prices are left to the free play of the competitive market, the prospects of profits decides what articles will be made, and in what quantities—and what articles will not be made at all. If there is no profit in making an article, it is a sign that the labor and capital devoted to its production are misdirected; the value of the resources that must be used up in making the article is greater than the value of the article itself.

"One function of profits, in brief, is to guide and channel the factors of production so as to apportion the relative output of thousands of different commodities in accordance with demand. No bureaucrat, no matter how brilliant, can solve this problem arbitrarily. Free prices and free profits will maximize production and relieve shortages quicker than any other system. Arbitrarily-fixed prices and arbitrarily-limited profits can only prolong shortages and reduce production and employment.

"Contrary to popular impression, profits are achieved not by raising prices, but by introducing economies and efficiencies that cut costs of production. It seldom happens (and unless there is a monopoly, it never happens over a long period) that *every* firm in an industry makes a profit. The price charged by all firms for the same commodity or service must be the same; those who try to charge a higher price do not find buyers. Therefore, the largest profits go to the firms that have achieved the lowest costs of production. These expand at the expense of the inefficient firms with higher costs. It is thus that the consumer and the public are served.

"Profits, in short, resulting from the relationships of costs to prices, not only tell us which goods it is most economical to make, but which are the most economical ways to make them. These questions must be answered by a socialist system no less than by a capitalist one; they must be answered by any conceivable economic system; and for the overwhelming bulk of the commodities and services that are produced, the answers supplied by profit and loss under competitive free enterprise are incomparably superior to those that could be obtained by any other method."

23. THE MIRAGE OF INFLATION

"Before we consider what the consequences of inflation are in specific cases, we should consider what its consequences are in general. Even prior to that, it seems desirable to ask why inflation has been constantly resorted to, why it has had an immemorial popular appeal, and why its siren music has tempted one nation after another down the path to economic disaster.

"The most obvious and yet the oldest and most stubborn error on which the appeal of inflation rests is that of confusing 'money' with wealth. To many the conclusion seems obvious that if the government merely issued more money and distributed it to everybody, we should all be that much richer.

"These are the most naive inflationists. There is a second group, less naive, who see that if the whole thing were as easy as that the government could solve all our problems merely by printing money. The more knowing inflationists recognize that any substantial increase in the quantity of money will reduce the purchasing power of each individual monetary unit––in other words, that it will lead to an increase in commodity prices."

Detailed examples show the steps by which inflation raises prices and it follows that: "Inflation turns out to be merely one more example of our central lesson. It may indeed bring benefits for a short time to favored groups, but only at the expense of others. And in the long run it brings ruinous consequences to the whole community. Even a relatively mild inflation distorts the structure of production. It leads to the over-expansion of some industries at the expense of others. This involves a misapplication and waste of capital.

"Nor is it possible to bring inflation to a smooth and gentle stop, and so avert a subsequent depression. It is not even possible to halt an inflation, once embarked upon, at some preconceived point, or when prices have achieved a previously-agreed-upon level; for both political and economic forces will have got out of hand. It is impossible, moreover, to control the value of money under inflation. The present valuation will often depend upon what people expect the *future* quantity of money to be. And, as with commodities on the speculative exchanges, each person's valuation of money is affected not only by what *he* thinks its value is but by what he thinks is going to be *everybody else's* valuation of money.

"All this explains why, when super-inflation has once set in, the value of the monetary unit drops at a far faster rate than the quantity of money either is or can be increased. When this stage is reached, the disaster is nearly complete; and the scheme is bankrupt.

"Yet the ardor for inflation never dies. It would almost seem as if no country is capable of profiting from the experience of another and no generation of learning from the suffering of its forebears. Each generation and country follows the same mirage. For it is the nature of inflation to give birth to a thousand illusions.

"What inflation really does is to change the relationships of prices and costs. The most important change it is designed to bring about is to raise commodity prices in relation to wage rates, and so to restore business profits, and encourage a resumption of output at the points where the idle resources exist, by restoring a workable relationship between prices and costs of production.

"It should be immediately clear that this could be brought about more directly and honestly by a reduction in unworkable wage rates. But the more sophisticated proponents of inflation believe that this is now politically impossible. Sometimes they go further, and charge that all proposals under any circumstances to reduce particular wage rates directly in order to reduce unemployment are 'anti-labor.' But what they are themselves proposing, stated in bald terms, is to *deceive* labor by reducing *real* wage rates (that is, wage rates in terms of purchasing power) through an increase in prices.

"Inflation is the opium of the people. And this is precisely its political function.

"Inflation does not and cannot affect everyone evenly. Some suffer more than others. The poor are usually more heavily taxed by inflation, in percentage terms, than the rich, for they do not have the same means of protecting themselves by speculative purchases of real equities.

"Like every other tax, inflation acts to determine the individual and business policies we all are forced to follow. It discourages all prudence and thrift. It encourages squandering, gambling, reckless waste of all kinds. It often makes it more profitable to speculate than to produce. It tears apart the whole fabric of stable economic relationships. Its inexcusable injustices drive men toward desperate remedies. It plants seeds of fascism and communism. It leads men to demand totalitarian controls. It ends invariably in bitter disillusion and collapse."

24. THE ASSAULT ON SAVING

"From time immemorial proverbial wisdom has taught the virtues of saving, and warned against the consequences of prodigality and waste. This proverbial wisdom has reflected the common ethical as well as the merely prudential judgments of mankind. But there have always been squanderers, and there have apparently always been theorists to rationalize their squandering.

"The classical economists, refuting the fallacies of their own day, showed that the saving policy that was in the best interests of the individual was also in the best interests of the nation. They showed that the rational saver, in making provision for his own future, was not hurting, but helping, the whole community."

Hazlitt outlines a parable by Bastiat telling of two brothers—–one spends his inheritance in riotous living while the other lives modestly, saves and invests. It appears that the big-spender is creating much more business but Bastiat shows that this is an illusion since actually the investor causes fully as much immediate business and his continues to increase while the other stops abruptly when he goes broke.

The difference between *hoarding* and *investing* is analyzed and it is determined that hoarding is really only deferred spending. "If they defer spending, they believe they will get more for their money. They do not wish to have their resources in goods that are falling in value, but in money which they expect (relatively) to rise in value.

"The same expectation prevents them from investing. They have lost their confidence in the profitability of business; or at least they believe that if they wait a few months they can buy bonds or stocks cheaper.

"It is a misnomer to call this temporary refusal to buy 'saving.' It does not spring from the same motives as normal saving. And it is a still more serious error to say that this sort of 'saving' is the *cause* of depression. It is, on the contrary, the *consequence* of depressions. It is true that this refusal to buy may intensify and prolong a depression once begun. But it does not itself originate the depression.

"Still another objection is made against saving. It is said to be just downright silly. The Nineteenth Century is derided for its supposed inculcation of the doctrine that mankind through saving should go on making itself a larger and larger cake without ever eating the cake. This picture of the process is itself naive and childish. It can best be disposed of, perhaps, by putting before ourselves a somewhat more realistic picture of what actually takes place."

A short tabulation shows what actually happens when 20% of production goes to capital goods which in turn increase total production by 2-½% per year. In eleven years the 80 (%) consumer goods has increased to 100 as total production rises from 100 to 125. It is important to note "that total production increases each year *because of the saving*, and would not have increased without it."

A clear explanation of the function of interest rates concludes with: "And just as the supply of and demand for any other commodity are equalized by price, so the supply of and demand for capital are equalized by interest rates. The interest rate is merely the special name for the price of loaned capital. It is a price like any other.

"This whole subject has been so appallingly confused in recent years by complicated sophistries and disastrous governmental policies based upon them that one almost despairs of getting back to common sense and sanity about it. There is a psychopathic fear of 'excessive' interest rates. It is argued that if interest rates are too high it will not be profitable for industry to borrow and invest in new plants and machines.

This argument has been so effective that governments everywhere in recent decades have pursued artificial 'cheap money' policies. But the argument, in its concern with increasing the demand for capital, overlooks the effect of these policies on the supply of capital. It is one more example of the fallacy of looking at the effects of a policy only on one group and forgetting the effects on another. If interest rates are artificially kept too low in relation to risks, there will be a reduction in both saving and lending.

"The effect of keeping interest rates artificially low, in fact, is eventually the same as that of keeping any other price below the natural market. It increases demand and reduces supply. It increases the demand for capital and reduces the supply of real capital. It creates economic distortions. It is true, no doubt, that an artificial reduction in the interest rate encourages increased borrowing. It tends, in fact, to encourage highly speculative ventures that cannot continue except under the artificial conditions that gave them birth. On the supply side, the artificial reduction of interest rates discourages normal thrift, saving, and investment. It reduces the accumulation of capital. It slows down the increase in productivity, that 'economic growth,' that 'progressives' profess to be so eager to promote.

"If no effort is made to tamper with money rates through inflationary governmental policies, increased savings create their own demand by lowering interest rates in a natural manner. The greater supply of savings seeking investment forces savers to accept lower rates. But lower rates also mean that more enterprises can afford to borrow because their prospective profit on the new machines or plants they buy with the proceeds seems likely to exceed what they have to pay for the borrowed funds."

25. THE LESSON RESTATED

"In seeing that economics is a science of tracing consequences, we must have become aware that, like logic and mathematics, it is a science of recognizing inevitable *implications*."

Hazlitt shows the similarity of inherent economic and mathematical implications, and continues: "In the same way the economist, assigned a practical problem, must know both the essential facts of that problem and the valid deductions to be drawn from those facts.

"Now few people recognize the necessary implications of the economic statements they are constantly making. When they say that the way of economic salvation is to increase 'credit,' it is just as if they said that the way to economic salvation is to increase debt; these are different names for the same thing seen from opposite sides. When they say that the way to prosperity is to increase farm prices, it is like saying that the way to prosperity is to make food dearer for the city worker. When they say that the way to national wealth is to pay out governmental subsidies, they are in effect saying that the way to national wealth is to increase taxes. When they make it a main objective to increase exports, most of them do not realize that they necessarily make it a main objective ultimately to increase imports. When they say, under nearly all conditions, that the way to recovery is to increase wage rates, they have found only another way of saying that the way to recovery is to increase costs of production.

"The analysis of our illustrations has taught us another incidental lesson. That is that, when we study the effects of various proposals, not merely on special groups in the short run, but on all groups in the long run, the conclusions we arrive at usually correspond with those of unsophisticated common sense. It would not occur to anyone not acquainted with the prevailing economic half-literacy that it is good to have windows broken and cities destroyed; that it is anything but waste to create needless public projects, that it is dangerous to let idle hordes of men return to work; that machines which increase the production of wealth and economize human effort are to be dreaded; that obstructions to free production and free consumption increase wealth; that a nation grows richer by forcing other nations to take its goods for less than they cost to produce; that saving is stupid or wicked and that squandering brings prosperity.

"It is certainly true, however, that a little economics can easily lead to the paradoxical and preposterous conclusions we have just rehearsed, but depth in economics brings men back to common sense. For depth in economics consists in looking for all the consequences of a policy instead of merely resting one's gaze on those immediately visible.

"Our study of our lesson would not be complete if, before we took leave of it, we neglected to observe that the fundamental fallacy with which we have been concerned arises not accidentally but systematically. It is an almost inevitable result, in fact, of the division of labor.

"In a primitive community, or among pioneers, before the division of labor has arisen, a man works solely for himself or his immediate family. What he consumes is identical with what he produces. There is always a direct and immediate connection between his output and his satisfactions.

"But when the elaborate and minute division of labor has set in, this direct and immediate connection ceases to exist. I do not make all the things I consume but, perhaps, only one of them. With the income I derive from making this one commodity, or rendering this one service, I buy all the rest."

Hazlitt continues with a discussion of limiting production in an attempt to raise prices, and he outlines the effects of new and improved machines––the specific harm to a few but the over-all good. "A new textile machine, weaving a better cloth at a faster rate, will make thousands of old machines obsolete, and wipe out part of the capital value invested in them, so making poorer the owners of those machines.

"Just as there is no technical improvement that would not hurt someone, so there is no change in public taste or morals, even for the better, that would not hurt someone. An increase in sobriety would put thousands of bartenders out of business. A decline in gambling would force croupiers and racing touts to seek more productive occupations.

"But it is not merely those who deliberately pander to men's vices who would be hurt by a sudden improvement in public morals. Among those who would be hurt most are precisely those whose business it is to improve those morals. Preachers would have less to complain about; reformers would lose their causes; the demand for their services and contributions for their support would decline. If there were no criminals we would need fewer lawyers, judges and firemen, and no jailers, no locksmiths, and (except for such services as untangling traffic snarls) even no policemen.

"Under a system of division of labor, in short, it is difficult to think of a greater fulfillment of any human need which would not, at least temporarily, hurt some of the people who have made investments or painfully acquired skill to meet that precise need. If progress were completely even all around the circle, this antagonism between the interests of the whole community and of the specialized group would not, if it were noticed at all, present any serious problem.

"But economic progress never has taken place and probably never will take place in this completely uniform way. Advance occurs now in this branch of production and now in that. And if there is a sudden increase in the supply of the thing I help to produce, or if a new invention or discovery makes what I produce no longer necessary, then the gain to the world is a tragedy to me and to the productive group to which I belong.

"Now it is often not the diffused gain of the increased supply or new discovery that most forcibly strikes even the disinterested observer, but the concentrated loss. But the solution is never to reduce supplies arbitrarily, to prevent further inventions or discoveries, or to support people for continuing to perform a service that has lost its value. Yet this is what the world has repeatedly sought to do by protective tariff, by the destruction of machinery, by the burning of coffee, by a thousand reduction schemes. This is the insane doctrine of wealth through scarcity.

"It is a doctrine that may always be privately true, unfortunately, for any particular group of producers considered in isolation––if they can make scarce the one thing they have to sell while keeping abundant all the things they have to buy. But it is a doctrine that is always publicly false. It can never be applied all around the circle. For its application would mean economic suicide.

"And this is our lesson in its most generalized form. For many things that seem to be true when we concentrate on a single economic group are seen to be illusions when the interests of everyone, as consumer no less than as producer, are considered.

"To see the problem as a whole, and not in fragments: that is the goal of economic science."

26. A NOTE ON BOOKS

Hazlitt concludes his intensely interesting book on economics with a couple of pages discussing other books on the subject; from simple primers to many popular works and on to a few deep technical treatises.

Before leaving the broad subject of economics it seems advisable to clarify the effect of inflation on interest rates.

Any individual or corporation engaging in leasing (whether an article, commodity or service) must set the schedule of charges to cover all of the basic costs of doing business. For leasing these costs are:

1. A charge for change of control––the right to use.
2. A charge for depreciation––any loss in value during lease.
3. A charge for possible theft or non-return, in whole or part.
4. A charge for business overhead––management, clerical, rent, utilities, etc.

These costs are obvious for automobile leasing where the basic daily rate covers items 1 and 4 plus a charge for insurance to cover item #3, and the mileage rate covers item 2, plus fuel, etc.

In the particular case of leasing money (lending) some costs are less well understood. Most loans have some collateral which eliminates any need of a charge for item 3, except in unstable societies as where a revolution may be expected to wipe out all indebtedness (and possibly the people also). With highly efficient business methods the charge for item 4 is only a small fraction of one percent per annum except for relatively small loans. (It costs as much to process a loan of $100 as one of $100,000 but the percentage cost is 1,000 times as much). Thus the "prime" rate of interest (i.e., the best rate for large amounts) is composed almost entirely of items 1 and 2.

Money does not depreciate in the sense that a worn dollar bill would have less value than a new one but under inflation all money depreciates to the extent that each dollar will purchase less a year later. The market value of item 1 (the charge for the right to use) depends largely upon the degree of capitalization of the society and may range from dozens or hundreds or even thousands[4] of percent per annum for totally uncapitalized societies down to below 1% for those highly capitalized. Historically the lowest interest rate in the U.S.A. was about 1½% early in this century. At that time there was negligible inflation, and without inflation it now should be about 1%, or slightly less, as our degree of capitalization is much greater. Thus a base rate now of 5% is really only about 1% true interest (i.e., the charge for the control of the money). The remaining 4% is simply a charge for inflation. This means that if you borrow $100 for a year at 5%, you pay back the $100 plus a charge of $1 for the use of the money, and $4 for inflation. Here both borrower and lender assumed that prices in general would advance about 4% during the year, so that the $104 repaid at the end of the year would purchase approximately what $100 would have purchased the year before.

If the U.S.A. continues its deficit financing the inflation must

---

[4] As an example consider an isolated farmer in a barter economy (i.e., no money) who has lost his supply of seed corn and thus faces starvation or the loss of his farm. His only possible supply of seed is from another farmer who has only sufficient seed to plant his own acreage and thus risks a similar fate if he loses his crop. After careful deliberation they agree to split the seed on the basis that the borrower return to the lender one-half of his total crop. This certainly is fair, with the borrower probably getting the best of the deal. Under these circumstances the corn would be planted in the most fertile soil and given the best of care to insure a maximum yield. If each kernel brought forth three or four ears of corn the return would be some 800 to 1500 kernels per kernel planted. Taking 1002 as a fair average, the half returned would be 501 kernels per kernel borrowed. Then the bonus, or interest, would be 500 to 1, for a half year loan, and the interest rate would be 500 times 100, or 50,000% for a half-year, corresponding to the rate of 100,000% per annum.

continue (as described on pages 71 and 128) and the total interest rate will move up in proportion. For the government to force inflation by loose financial policies and still try to hold down interest rates (as if there were no connection) is quite comparable to a steam boiler operator who pours fuel to the fire but also holds down the safety valve and gives full assurance that all is well.

THE ROAD TO SERFDOM

We have concluded our discussion of economic fallacies and we shall now look at the result which must follow the continued acceptance of these fallacies. *The Road to Serfdom*, by Friedrich A. Hayek, published in 1944 by The University of Chicago Press, is a highly penetrating analysis. It was condensed in and reprinted by *The Reader's Digest*; and we have further condensed that condensation here to emphasize the points most pertinent to this study.

FOREWORD

"The author is an internationally known economist. An Austrian by birth, he was director of the Austrian Institute for Economic Research and lecturer in economics at the University of Vienna during the years of the rise of fascism in central Europe.

"Professor Hayek, with great power and rigor of reasoning, sounds a grim warning to Americans and Britons who look to the government to provide the way out of all our economic difficulties. He demonstrates that fascism and what the Germans correctly call National Socialism are the inevitable results of the increasing growth of state control and state power, of national 'planning' and of socialism.

"In a foreword to *The Road to Serfdom*, John Chamberlain, book editor of *Harper's*, writes: 'This book is a warning cry in a time of hesitation. It says to us: Stop, look and listen. Its logic is incontestable, and it should have the widest possible audience.'"

The Road to Serfdom

"The very magnitude of the outrages committed by the National Socialists has strengthened the assurance that a totalitarian system cannot happen here. But let us remember that 15 years ago [about 1930] the possibility of such a thing happening in Germany would have appeared just as fantastic not only to nine-tenths of the Germans themselves but also to the most hostile foreign observer.

"There are many features which were then regarded as 'typically German' which now are equally familiar in America and England, and many symptoms that point to a further development in the same direction: the increasing veneration for the state, the fatalistic acceptance of 'inevitable trends,' the enthusiasm for 'organization' of everything (we now call it 'planning').

"The character of the danger is, if possible, even less understood here than it was in Germany. The supreme tragedy is still not seen that in Germany it was largely people of good will who, by their socialist policies, prepared the way for the forces which stand for everything they detest. *Few recognize that the rise of fascism and Nazism was not a reaction against the socialist trends of the preceding period but a necessary outcome of those tendencies.*

"In the democracies at present, many who sincerely hate all of Nazism's manifestations are working for ideals whose realization would lead straight to the abhorred tyranny. Most of the people whose views influence developments are in some measure socialists. They believe that our economic life should be 'consciously directed,' that we should substitute 'economic planning' for the competitive system. Yet is there a greater tragedy imaginable than that, in our endeavor to consciously shape our future in accordance with high ideals, we should in fact unwittingly produce the very opposite of what we have been striving for?"

PLANNING AND POWER

"In order to achieve their ends, the planners must create power—power over men wielded by other men—of a magnitude never before known. Their success will depend upon the extent to which they achieve such power.

"Many socialists have the tragic illusion that by depriving private individuals of the power they possess in an individualist system, and transferring this power to society, they thereby extinguish power. What they overlook is that, by concentrating power so that it can be used in the service of a single plan, it is not merely transformed but infinitely heightened. By uniting in the hands of some single body power formerly exercised independently by many, an amount of power is created infinitely greater than any that existed before, so much more far-reaching as almost to be different in kind.

"It is fallacious to argue that the great power exercised by a central planning board would be 'no greater than the power collectively exercised by private boards of directors.' There is in a competitive society, nobody who can exercise even a fraction of the power which a socialist planning board would possess. To decentralize power is to reduce the absolute amount of power, and the competitive system is the only system designed to minimize the power exercised by man over man. Who can seriously doubt that the power which a millionaire, who may be my employer, has over me is very much less than that which the smallest bureaucrat possesses who wields the coercive power of the state and on whose discretion it depends how I am allowed to live and work?

"Our generation has forgotten that the system of private property is the most important guarantee of freedom. It is only because the control of the means of production is divided among many people acting independently that we as individuals can decide what to do with ourselves. When all the means of production are vested in a single hand, whether it be nominally that of 'society' as a whole or that of a dictator, whoever exercises this control has complete power over us. In the hands of private individuals, what is called economic power can be an instrument of coercion, but it is never control over the whole life of a person. But when economic power is centralized as an instrument of political power it creates a degree of dependence scarcely distinguishable from slavery. It has been well said, that in a country where the sole employer is the state, opposition means death by slow starvation."

Background to Danger

"Individualism, in contrast to socialism and all other forms of totalitarianism, is based on the respect of Christianity for the individual man and the belief that it is desirable that men should be free to develop their own individual gifts and bents. This philosophy, first fully developed during the Renaissance, grew and spread into what we know as Western civilization.

"Perhaps the greatest results of this unchaining of individual energies was the marvelous growth of science. Only since industrial freedom opened the path to the free use of new knowledge, only since everything could be tried——if somebody could be found to back it at his own risk——has science made the great strides which in the last 150 years have changed the face of the world. The result of this growth surpassed all expectations. Wherever the barriers to the free exercise of human ingenuity were removed, man became rapidly able to satisfy ever-widening ranges of desire. By the beginning of the 20th century the workingman in the Western World had reached a degree of material comfort, security and personal independence which 100 years before had hardly seemed possible.

"The effect of this success was to create among men a new sense of power over their own fate, the belief in the unbounded possibilities of improving their own lot. What had been achieved came to be regarded as a secure and imperishable possession, acquired once and for all; and the rate of progress began to seem too slow. MOREOVER, THE PRINCIPLES WHICH HAD MADE THIS PROGRAM POSSIBLE CAME TO BE REGARDED AS OBSTACLES TO SPEEDIER PROGRESS, IMPATIENTLY TO BE BRUSHED AWAY.

"No sensible person should have doubted that the economic

principles of the 19th century were only a beginning——that there were immense possibilities of advancement on the lines on which we had moved. But according to the views now dominant, the question is no longer how we can make the best use of the spontaneous forces found in a free society. We have in effect undertaken to dispense with these forces and to replace them by collective and 'conscious' direction.

"It is significant that this abandonment of liberalism, whether expressed as socialism in its more radical form or merely as 'organization' or 'planning,' was perfected in Germany. The Germans, long before the Nazis, were attacking liberalism and democracy, capitalism and individualism. By the time Hitler came to power, liberalism was dead in Germany. And it was socialism that had killed it.

"To many who have watched the transition from socialism to fascism at close quarters the connection between the two systems has become increasingly obvious, but in the democracies the majority of people still believe that socialism and freedom can be combined. They do not realize that democratic socialism, the great utopia of the last few generations, is not only unachievable but that to strive for it produces something utterly different——the very destruction of freedom itself. As has been aptly said: 'What has always made the state a hell on earth has been precisely that man has tried to make it his heaven.'

"It is disquieting to see in England and the United States today the same drawing together of forces and nearly the same contempt of all that is liberal in the old sense. 'Conservative socialism' was the slogan under which a large number of writers prepared the atmosphere in which National Socialism succeeded. It is 'conservative socialism' which is the dominant trend among us now."

The Liberal Way of Planning
The Great Utopia

"Nobody saw more clearly than the great political thinker de Tocqueville that democracy stands in an irreconcilable conflict with socialism: 'Democracy attaches all possible value to each man,' he said in 1848, 'while socialism makes each man a mere agent, a mere number.

Democracy and socialism have nothing in common but one word: equality. But notice the difference: while democracy seeks equality in liberty, socialism seeks equality in restraint and servitude.'

"To allay these suspicions and to harness to its cart the strongest of all political motives––the craving for freedom––socialists began increasingly to make use of the promise of a 'new freedom.' Socialism was to bring 'economic freedom,' without which political freedom was 'not worth having.'

"To make this argument sound plausible, the word 'freedom' was subjected to a subtle change in meaning. The word had formerly meant freedom from coercion, from the arbitrary power of other men. Now it was made to mean freedom from necessity, release from the compulsion of the circumstances which inevitably limit the range of choice of all of us. Freedom in this sense is, of course, merely another name for power or wealth. The demand for the new freedom was thus only another name for a redistribution of wealth.

"The claim that a planned economy would produce a substantially larger output than the competitive system is being progressively abandoned by most students of the problem. Yet it is this false hope as much as anything which drives us along the road to planning.

"WHAT IS PROMISED TO US AS THE ROAD TO FREEDOM IS IN FACT THE HIGH ROAD TO SERVITUDE. For it is not difficult to see what must be the consequences when democracy embarks upon a course of planning. The goal of the planning will be described by some such vague term as 'the general welfare.'

"Democratic assemblies cannot function as planning agencies. They cannot produce agreements on everything––the whole direction of the resources of the nation––for the number of possible courses of action will be legion. Even if Congress could, by proceeding step-by-step and compromising at each point, agree on some scheme, it would certainly in the end satisfy nobody.

"Thus the legislative body will be reduced to choosing the persons who are to have practically absolute power. The whole system will tend toward that kind of dictatorship in which the head of the government is from time to time confirmed in his position by popular vote, but where HE HAS ALL THE POWERS AT HIS COMMAND TO MAKE CERTAIN THAT THE VOTE WILL GO IN THE DIRECTION HE DESIRES.

"Individual freedom cannot be reconciled with the supremacy of one single purpose to which the whole of society is permanently subordinated.

"To those who have watched the transition from socialism to fascism at close quarters, the connection between the two systems is obvious. The realization of the socialist program means the destruction of freedom. Democratic socialism, the great utopia of the last few generations, is simply not achievable."

Why the Worst Get on Top

"Just as the democratic statesman who sets out to plan economic life will soon be confronted with the alternative of either assuming dictatorial powers or abandoning his plans, so the totalitarian leader would soon have to choose between disregard of ordinary morals and failure. It is for this reason that the unscrupulous are likely to be more successful in a society tending toward totalitarianism. Who does not see this has not yet grasped the full width of the gulf which separates totalitarianism from the essentially individualist Western civilization.

"The totalitarian leader must collect around him a group which is prepared voluntarily to submit to that discipline which they are to impose by force upon the rest of the people.

"That socialism can be put into practice only by methods which most socialists disapprove is, of course, a lesson learned by many social reformers in the past. Others had already learned the lesson that in a planned society the question can no longer be on what do a majority of the people agree but what the largest single group is whose members agree sufficiently to make unified direction of all affairs possible.

"There are three main reasons why such a numerous group, with fairly similar views, is not likely to be formed by the best but rather by the worst elements of any society.

"First, the higher the education and intelligence of individuals become, the more their tastes and views are differentiated. If we wish to find a high degree of uniformity in outlook, we have to descend to the regions of lower moral and intellectual standards where the more primitive instincts prevail. This does not mean that the majority of people have low moral standards; it merely means that the largest group of people whose values are very similar are the people with low standards.

"Second, since this group is not large enough to give sufficient weight to the leader's endeavors, he will have to increase their numbers by converting more to the same simple creed. He must gain the support of the docile and gullible, who have no strong convictions of their own but are ready to accept a ready-made system of values if it is only drummed into their ears sufficiently loudly and frequently. It will be those whose vague and imperfectly formed ideas are easily swayed and whose passions and emotions are readily aroused who will thus swell the ranks of the totalitarian party.

"Third, to weld together a closely coherent body of supporters, the leader must appeal to a common human weakness. It seems to be easier for people to agree on a negative program—on the hatred of an enemy, on envy of those better off—than on any positive task.

"The contrast between the 'we' and the 'they' is consequently always employed by those who seek the allegiance of huge masses. The enemy may be internal, like the 'Jew' in Germany or the 'kulak' in Russia, or he may be external. In any case, this technique has the great advantage of leaving the leader greater freedom of action than would almost any positive program.

"Advancement within a totalitarian group or party depends largely on a willingness to do immoral things. The principle that the end justifies the means, which in individual ethics is regarded as the denial of all morals, in collectivist ethics becomes necessarily the supreme rule. There is literally nothing which the consistent collectivist must not be prepared to do if it serves 'the good of the whole.' Because that is to him the only criterian of what ought to be done.

"Once you admit that the individual is merely a means to serve the ends of the higher entity called society or the nation, most of the features of totalitarianism which horrify us follow of necessity. From the collectivist standpoint intolerance and brutal suppression of dissent, deception and spying, the complete disregard of the life and happiness of the individual are essential and unavoidable. Acts which revolt our feelings, such as the shooting of hostages or the killing of the old or sick, are treated as mere matters of expediency; the compulsory uprooting and transportation of hundreds of thousands becomes an instrument of policy approved by almost everybody except the victims.

"To be a useful assistant in the running of a totalitarian state, therefore, a man must be prepared to break every moral rule he has ever known if this seems necessary to achieve the end set for him. In the totalitarian machine there will be special opportunities for the ruthless and unscrupulous.

"A further point should be made here:

> Collectivism means the end of truth. To make a totalitarian system function efficiently, it is not enough that everybody should be forced to work for the ends selected by those in control; it is essential that the people should come to regard these ends as their own. This is brought about by propaganda and by complete control of all sources of information.

"The most effective way of making people accept the validity of the values they are to serve is to persuade them that they are really the same as those they have always held, but which were not properly understood or recognized before. And the most efficient technique to this end is to use the old words but change their meaning. Few traits of totalitarian regimes are at the same time so confusing to the superficial observer and yet so characteristic of the whole intellectual climate as this complete perversion of language.

"The worst sufferer in this respect is the word 'liberty.' It is a word used as freely in totalitarian states as elsewhere. Indeed, it could almost be said that wherever liberty as we know it has been destroyed, this has been done in the name of some new freedom promised to the people. Even among us we have planners who promise us a 'collective freedom,' which is as misleading as anything said by totalitarian politicians. 'Collective freedom' is not the freedom of the members of society but the unlimited freedom of the planner to do with society that which he pleases. This is the confusion of freedom with power carried to the extreme.

"It is not difficult to deprive the majority of independent thought. But the minority who will retain an inclination to criticize must also be silenced. Public criticism or even expressions of doubt must be suppressed because they tend to weaken support of the regime.

"*Every* activity must derive its justification from conscious social purpose. There must be no spontaneous, unguided activity, because it might produce results which cannot be foreseen and for which the plan does not provide.

"Perhaps the most alarming fact is that contempt for intellectual liberty is not a thing which arises only once the totalitarian system is established but can be found everywhere among those who have embraced a collectivist faith. The worst oppression is condoned if it is committed in the name of socialism. Intolerance of opposing ideas is openly extolled. *The tragedy of collectivist thought is that, while it starts out to make reason supreme, it ends by destroying reason.*

"There is one aspect of the change in moral values brought about by the advance of collectivism which provides special food for thought. It is that the virtues which are held less and less in esteem in Britain and America are precisely those on which Anglo-Saxons justly prided themselves and in which they were generally recognized to excel. These virtues are independence and self-reliance, individual initiative and local responsibility, the successful reliance on voluntary activity, noninterference with one's neighbor and tolerance of the different, and a healthy suspicion of power and authority.

"Almost all the traditions and institutions which have molded the national character and the whole moral climate of England and

America are those which the progress of collectivism and its centralistic tendencies are progressively destroying."

Planning vs. the Rule of Law

"Nothing distinguishes more clearly a free country from a country under arbitrary government than the observance in the former of the great principles known as the Rule of Law. Stripped of technicalities, this means that government in all its actions is bound by rules fixed and announced beforehand––rules that make it possible to foresee with fair certainty how the authority will use its coercive powers in given circumstances and to plan one's individual affairs on the basis of this knowledge. Thus, within the known rules of the game, the individual is free to pursue his personal ends, certain that the powers of government will not be used deliberately to frustrate his efforts.

"Socialist economic planning necessarily involves the very opposite of this. The planning authority cannot tie itself down in advance to general rules which prevent arbitrariness.

"When the government has to decide how many pigs are to be raised or how many buses are to run, which coal mines are to operate, or at what prices shoes are to be sold, these decisions cannot be settled for long periods in advance. They depend inevitably on the circumstances of the moment, and in making such decisions it will always be necessary to balance, one against the other, the interests of various persons and groups.

"In the end somebody's views will have to decide whose interests are more important, and these views must become part of the law of the land. Hence, the familiar fact that the more the state 'plans,' the more difficult planning becomes for the individual.

"The difference between the two kinds of rules is important. It is the same as that between providing signposts and commanding which road to take.

"Moreover, under central planning the government cannot be impartial. The state ceases to be a piece of utilitarian machinery intended to help individuals in the fullest development of their individual personality and becomes an institution which deliberately discriminates between particular needs of different people, and allows one man to do what another man must be prevented from doing.

"The Rule of Law, the absence of legal privileges of particular people designated by authority, is what safeguards that equality before the law which is the opposite of arbitrary government.

"In a planned society the law must legalize what to all intents and purposes remains arbitrary action. If the law says that such a board or authority may do what it pleases, anything that board or authority does is legal––but its actions are certainly not subject to the Rule of Law.

"By giving the government unlimited powers, the most arbitrary rule can be made legal: and in this way a democracy may set up the most complete despotism imaginable."

Is Planning Inevitable?

"One argument frequently heard is that the complexity of modern civilization creates new problems with which we cannot hope to deal effectively except by central planning. This argument is based upon a complete misapprehension of the working of competition. The very complexity of modern conditions makes competition the *only* method by which a coordination of affairs can be adequately achieved.

"Under competition––and under no other economic order––the price system automatically records all the relevant data. Entrepreneurs, by watching the movement of comparatively few dials, can adjust their activities to those of their fellows.

"Compared with this method of solving the economic problem–– by decentralization plus automatic coordination through the price system––the method of central direction is incredibly clumsy, primitive, and limited in scope. Modern civilization has been possible precisely because it did not have to be consciously created. The division of labor has gone far beyond what could have been planned. Any further growth in economic complexity, far from making central direction more necessary, makes it more important than ever that we should use the technique of competition and not depend on conscious control."

Can Planning Free Us from Care?

"Most planners who have seriously considered the practical aspects of their task have little doubt that a directed economy must be run on dictatorial lines, that the complex system of interrelated activities must be directed by a staff of experts, with ultimate power in the hands of a commander-in-chief whose actions must not be fettered by democratic procedure. The consolation our planners offer us is that this authoritarian direction will apply 'only' to economic matters. This assurance is usually accompanied by the suggestion that, by giving up freedom in the less important aspects of our lives, we shall obtain freedom in the pursuit of higher values. On this ground people who abhor the idea of a political dictatorship often clamor for a dictator in the economic field.

"The arguments used appeal to our best instincts. If planning really did free us from less important cares and so made it easier to render our existence one of plain living and high thinking, who would wish to belittle such an ideal?

"Unfortunately, purely economic ends cannot be separated from the other ends of life. What is misleadingly called the 'economic motive' means merely the desire for general opportunity. If we strive for money, it is because money offers us the widest choice in enjoying the fruits of our efforts—once earned we are free to spend the money as we wish.

"Because it is through the limitation of our money incomes that we feel the restrictions which our relative poverty still imposes on us, many have come to hate money as the symbol of these restrictions. Actually, money is one of the greatest instruments of freedom ever invented by man. It is money which in existing society opens an astounding range of choice to the poor man—a range greater than that which not many generations ago was open to the wealthy.

"We shall better understand the significance of the service of money if we consider what it would really mean if, as so many socialists characteristically propose, the 'pecuniary motive' were largely displaced by 'non-economic incentives.' If all rewards, instead of being offered in money, were offered in the form of public distinctions, or privileges, positions of power over other men, better housing or food, opportunities for travel or education, this would merely mean that the recipient would no longer be allowed to choose, and that whoever fixed the reward would determine not only its size but the way in which it should be enjoyed.

"The so-called economic freedom which the planners promise us means precisely that we are to be relieved of the necessity of solving our own economic problems and that the bitter choices this often involves are to be made for us. Since under modern conditions we are for almost everything dependent on means which our fellow men provide, economic planning would involve direction of almost the whole of our life. There is hardly an aspect of it, from our primary needs to our relations with our family and friends, from the nature of our work to the use of our leisure, over which the planner would not exercise his 'conscious control.'

"Our freedom of choice in a competitive society rests on the fact that, if one person refuses to satisfy our wishes, we can turn to another. But if we face a monopolist we are at his mercy. And an authority directing the whole economic system would be the most powerful monopolist imaginable.

"The will of the authority would shape and 'guide' our daily lives even more in our position as producers. For most of us the time we spend at our work is a large part of our whole lives, and our job usually determines the place where and the people among whom we live. Hence, some freedom in choosing our work is probably even more important for our happiness than freedom to spend our income during our hours of leisure.

"Even in the best of worlds this freedom will be limited. Few people ever have an abundance of choice of occupation. But what matters is that we have some choice, that we are not absolutely tied to a job which has been chosen for us, and that if one position becomes intolerable, or if we set our heart on another, there is almost always a way for the able, at some sacrifice, to achieve this goal. Nothing makes conditions more unbearable than the knowledge that no effort of ours can change them. It may be bad to be just a cog in a machine but it is infinitely worse if we can no longer leave it, if we are tied to our place and to the superiors who have been chosen for us.

"In a competitive society most things can be had at a price. It is often a cruelly high price. We must sacrifice one thing to obtain another. The alternative, however, is not freedom of choice, but orders and prohibitions which must be obeyed.

"And it is indisputable that, if we want consciously to decide who is to have what, we must plan the whole economic system. But the question remains whether the price we should have to pay for the realization of somebody's ideal of justice is not bound to be more discontent and more oppression than was ever caused by the much-abused free play of economic forces.

"It is often said that political freedom is meaningless without economic freedom. This is true enough, but in a sense almost opposite from that in which the phrase is used by our planners. The economic freedom which is the prerequisite of any other freedom cannot be the freedom from economic care which the socialists promise us and which can be obtained only by relieving us of the power of choice. It must be that freedom of economic activity, which together with the right of choice, carries also the risk and responsibility of that right."

Two Kinds of Security

"In England and America special privileges, especially in the form of the 'regulation' of competition, the 'stabilization' of particular prices and wages, have assumed increasing importance.

"The general endeavor to achieve security by restrictive measures, supported by the state, has in the course of time produced a progressive transformation of society—a transformation in which, as in so many other ways, Germany has led and the other countries have followed. This development has been hastened by another effect of socialist teaching, the deliberate disparagement of all activities involving economic risk and the moral opprobrium cast on the gains which make risks worth taking but which only few can win.

"We cannot blame our young men when they prefer the safe, salaried position to the risk of enterprise after they have heard from their earliest youth the former described as the superior, more unselfish and disinterested occupation. The younger generation of today has grown up in a world in which, in school and press, the spirit of commercial enterprise has been represented as disreputable and the making of profit as immoral, where to employ 100 people is represented as exploitation but to command the same number is honorable.

"The conflict with which we have to deal is a fundamental one between two irreconcilable types of social organization, which have often been described as the commercial and the military. In either, both choice and risk rest with the individual or he is relieved of both. In the army, work and worker alike are allotted by authority, and this is the only system in which the individual can be conceded full economic security. This security, however, is inseparable from the restrictions on liberty and the hierarchical order of military life––it is the security of the barracks.

"In a society used to freedom it is unlikely that many people would be ready deliberately to purchase security at this price. But the policies which are followed now are nevertheless rapidly creating conditions in which the striving for security tends to become stronger than the love of freedom.

"If we are not to destroy individual freedom, competition must be left to function unobstructed. It is essential that we should relearn frankly to face the fact that freedom can be had only at a price and that as individuals we must be prepared to make severe material sacrifices to preserve it.

"We must regain the conviction on which liberty in the Anglo-Saxon countries has been based and which Benjamin Franklin expressed in a phrase applicable to us as individuals no less than as nations:

'Those who would give up essential liberty to purchase a little temporary safety deserve neither liberty nor safety.'"

Toward a Better World

"To build a better world, we must have the courage to make a new start. We must clear away the obstacles with which human folly has recently encumbered our path and release the creative energy of individuals. We must create conditions favorable to progress rather than 'planning progress.'

"The guiding principle in any attempt to create a world of free men must be this: A policy of freedom for the individual is the only truly progressive policy."

THE LAW

The essence of this study is that the modern "Conservative" is a conservative simply because he has some depth of understanding of the evil long-range effects inherent in most "liberal" proposals. The final great evil usually is camouflaged by a temporary benefit, and we started the analysis of this delayed reversal by quoting from a century old essay by Frederic Bastiat. The analysis was continued with examples and discussion from other basic books but it cannot be complete without reference to *The Law*, also by Bastiat, as that little treatise outlines the foundation on which all constructive thinking is based. Many scholars consider it the most fundamental book since the Bible and some, with long lists of earned degrees, read it regularly to deepen and refresh their understanding and inspiration.

The Law is so concise and beautifully written that any condensation would be an impertinence so we shall merely quote a few paragraphs and sentences and urge everyone to read and study the whole 60-page essay. All subheadings are shown even when we have no quote or comment in this condensation.

BASIC CONCEPT

"The law perverted! And the police powers of the state perverted along with it! The law, I say, not only turned from its proper purpose but made to

follow an entirely contrary purpose! The law become the weapon of every kind of greed! Instead of checking crime, the law itself guilty of the evils it is supposed to punish!"

Life is a Gift from God

"We hold from God the gift which includes all others. This gift is life––physical, intellectual, and moral life.

"But life cannot maintain itself alone. The Creator of life has entrusted us with the responsibility of preserving, developing, and perfecting it. In order that we may accomplish this, He has provided us with a collection of marvelous faculties. And He has put us in the midst of a variety of natural resources. By the application of our faculties to these natural resources we convert them into products and use them. This process is necessary in order that life may run its appointed course.

"Life, liberty and property do not exist because men have made laws. On the contrary, it was the fact that life, liberty and property existed beforehand that caused man to make laws in the first place."

What is Law?

"What, then, is law? It is the collective organization of the individual right to lawful defense.

"Each of us has a natural right––from God––to defend his person, his liberty, and his property. These are the three basic requirements of life, and the preservation of any one of them is completely dependent upon the preservation of the other two. For what are our faculties but the extension of our individuality. And what is property but an extension of our faculties.

"If every person has the right to defend––even by force––his person, his liberty, and his property, then it follows that a group of men have the right to organize and support a common force to protect these rights constantly. Thus the principle of collective rights––its reason for existing, its lawfulness––is based on individual right. And the common force that protects this collective right cannot logically have any other purpose or any other mission than that for which it acts as a substitute. Thus, since an individual cannot lawfully use force against the person, liberty, or property of another individual, then the common force——for the same reason——cannot lawfully be used to destroy the person, liberty, or property of individuals or groups.

"If this is true, then nothing can be more evident than this: The law is the organization of the natural right of lawful defense. It is the substitution of a common force for individual forces. And this common force is to do only what the individual forces have a natural and lawful right to do: to protect persons, liberties, and properties; to maintain the right of each, and to cause *justice* to reign over us all."

A Just and Enduring Government

"If a nation were founded on this basis, it seems to me that order would prevail among the people, in thought as well as in deed. Under such an administration, everyone would understand that he possessed all the privileges as well as all the responsibilities of his existence. It can be further stated, that thanks to the nonintervention of the state in private affairs, our wants and their satisfactions would develop themselves in a logical manner."

The Complete Perversion of the Law

"But unfortunately, law by no means confines itself to its proper functions. The law has gone further than this; it has acted in direct opposition to its own purposes.

"How has this perversion of the law been accomplished? And what has been the result?

"The law has been perverted by the influence of two entirely different causes: **stupid greed** and **false philanthropy.** Let us speak of the first.

STUPID GREED

A Fatal Tendency of Mankind

"Self-preservation and self-development are common aspirations among all people. And if everyone enjoyed the unrestricted use of his faculties and the free disposition of the fruits of his labor, social progress would be ceaseless, uninterrupted, and unfailing."

Property and Plunder

"Man can live and satisfy his wants only by ceaseless labor; by the ceaseless application of his faculties to natural resources. This process is the origin of property.

"But it is also true that a man may live and satisfy his wants by seizing and consuming the product of the labor of others. This process is the origin of plunder.

"Now since man is naturally inclined to avoid pain––and since labor is pain in itself––it follows that men will resort to plunder whenever plunder is easier than work. History shows this quite clearly. It is evident then that the proper purpose of law is to use the power of its collective force to stop this fatal tendency to plunder instead of to work. All the measures of the law should protect property and punish plunder."

"But generally, the law is made by one man or one class of men. This fact, combined with the fatal tendency that exists in the heart of man to satisfy his wants with the least possible effort, explains the almost universal perversion of the law."

Victims of Lawful Plunder

"Men naturally rebel against the injustice of which they are victims. Thus, when plunder is organized by law for the profit of those who make the law, all the plundered classes try somehow to enter––by peaceful or revolutionary means––into the making of laws. According to their degree of enlightenment, these plundered classes may propose one of two entirely different purposes when they attempt to attain political power: Either they may wish to stop lawful plunder, or they may wish to share it.

"Woe to the nation when this latter purpose prevails among the mass victims of lawful plunder when they, in turn, seize the power to make laws.

"Until that happens, the few practice lawful plunder upon the many, a common practice where the right to participate in making the law is limited to a few persons. But then, participation in the making of law becomes universal. And then, men seek to balance their conflicting interests by universal plunder. Instead of rooting out the injustices found in society, they make these injustices general."

The Results of Legal Plunder

"It is impossible to introduce into society a greater change and a greater evil than this: the conversion of the law into an instrument of plunder.

"What are the consequences of such a perversion? It would require volumes to describe them all. Thus we must content ourselves with pointing out the most striking.

"In the first place, it erases from everyone's conscience the distinction between justice and injustice.

"No society can exist unless the laws are respected to a certain degree. *The safest way to make laws respected is to make them respectable.* When law and morality contradict each other, the citizen has the cruel alternative of either losing his moral sense or losing his respect for the law.

"The nature of law is to maintain justice. This is so much the case that, in the minds of the people, law and justice are one and the same thing. There is in all of us a strong disposition to believe that anything lawful is also proper. This belief is so widespread that many persons have erroneously held that things are 'just' because law makes them so. Thus, in order to make plunder appear just and sacred to many consciences, it is only necessary for the law to decree and sanction it.

The Fate of Nonconformists

Bastiat discusses the disparagement of all who criticize such perverted laws and adds that:

"Another effect of this tragic perversion of the law is that it gives an exaggerated importance to political passions and conflicts, and to politics in general."

Who Shall Judge?

He then discusses universal suffrage, which was just becoming popular when this was written in 1850, and concludes that it means "universal suffrage for those who are capable."

The Reason Why Voting is Restricted

The motive is that the elector or voter does not exercise the right for himself alone, but for everybody. "The most extended elective system and the most restricted elective system are alike in this respect. They differ only in respect to what constitutes incapacity. It is not a difference of principle, but merely of degree. And why is incapacity a motive for exclusion? Because it is not the voter alone who suffers the consequences of his vote; because each vote touches and affects everyone in the entire community; because the people in the community have a right to demand some safeguards concerning the acts upon which their welfare and existence depend."

The Answer is to Restrict the Law

Bastait suggests that all the furor over voting rights "would lose nearly all of its importance if the law had always been what it ought to be.

"In fact, if law were restricted to protecting all persons, all liberties, and all properties; if law were nothing more than the organized combination of the individual's right to self-defense; if law were the obstacle, the check, the punisher of all oppression and plunder—is it likely that we citizens would then argue much about the extent of the franchise?

"Under these circumstances, is it likely that the extent of the right to vote would endanger that supreme good, the public peace? Is it likely that the excluded classes would refuse to peaceably await the coming of their right to vote?

"If the law were confined to its proper functions, everyone's interest in the law would be the same. Is it not clear that, under these circumstances, those who voted could not inconvenience those who did not vote?"

The Fatal Idea of Legal Plunder

"But on the other hand, imagine that this fatal principle has been introduced: Under the pretense of organization, regulation, protection, or encouragement, the law takes property from one person and gives it to another; the law takes the wealth of all and gives it to a few––whether farmers, manufacturers, shipowners, artists, or comedians. Under these circumstances, then certainly every class will aspire to grasp the law, and logically so."

"The excluded classes will furiously demand their right to vote–– and will overthrow society rather than not to obtain it. Even beggars and vagabonds will then prove to you that they also have an incontestable title to vote."

Perverted Law Causes Conflict

"As long as it is admitted that the law may be diverted from its true purpose––that it may violate property instead of protecting it––then everyone will want to participate in making the law, either to protect himself against plunder or to use it for plunder. Political questions will always be prejudicial, dominant, and all-absorbing."

Slavery and Tariffs under Plunder

Two Kinds of Plunder

The Law Defends Plunder

"Sometimes the law defends plunder and participates in it. Thus the beneficiaries are spared the shame, danger, and scruple which their acts would otherwise involve. Sometimes the law places the whole apparatus of judges, police, prisons, and gendarmes at the service of the plunderers, and treats the victim––when he defends himself––as a criminal. In short, there is a *legal plunder*."

How to Identify Legal Plunder

"But how is this legal plunder to be identified? Quite simply. See if the law takes from some persons what belongs to them, and gives it to other persons to whom it does not belong. See if the law benefits one citizen at the expense of another by doing what the citizen himself cannot do without committing a crime."

Legal Plunder Has Many Names

"Now legal plunder can be committed in an infinite number of ways. Thus we have an infinite number of plans for organizing it: tariffs, protection, benefits, subsidies, encouragements, progressive taxation, public schools, guaranteed jobs, guaranteed profits, minimum wages, a right to relief, a right to the tools of labor, free credit, and so on, and so on. All these plans as a whole––with their common aim of legal plunder––constitute socialism."

Socialism is Legal Plunder

The Choice Before Us

"The question of legal plunder must be settled once and for all, and there are only three ways to settle it:

1. The few plunder the many.
2. Everybody plunders everybody.
3. Nobody plunders anybody.

No legal plunder: This is the principal of justice, peace, order, stability, harmony, and logic."

The Proper Function of the Law

"And, in all sincerity, can anything more than the absence of plunder be required of the law? Can the law––which necessarily requires the use of force––rationally be used for anything except protecting the rights of everyone? I defy anyone to extend it beyond this purpose without perverting it and, consequently, turning might against right. This is the most fatal and most illogical social perversion that can possibly be imagined. It must be admitted that the true solution––so long searched for in the area of social relationships––is contained in these simple words: Law is organized Justice.

"Now this must be said: When justice is organized by law––that is, by force––this excludes the idea of using law (force) to organize any human activity whatever, whether it be labor, charity, agriculture, commerce, industry, education, art, or religion. The organizing by law of any one of these would inevitably destroy the essential organization––Justice."

FALSE PHILANTHROPY

The Indirect Approach to Despotism

"Here I encounter the most popular fallacy of our times. It is not considered sufficient that the law should be just; it must be philanthropic. Nor is it sufficient that the law should guarantee to every citizen the free and inoffensive use of his faculties for physical, intellectual, and moral self-improvement. Instead, it is demanded that the law should directly extend welfare, education, and morality throughout the nation.

"This is the seductive lure of socialism. And I repeat again: These two uses of the law are in direct contradiction to each other. We must choose between them. A citizen cannot at the same time be free and not free."

Enforced Fraternity Destroys Liberty

"In fact, it is impossible for me to separate the word fraternity from the word voluntary. I cannot possibly understand how fraternity can be legally enforced without liberty being legally destroyed, and thus justice being legally trampled underfoot."

Plunder Violates Ownership

"I do not mean to attack the intentions or the morality of anyone. Rather, I am attacking an *idea* which I believe to be false; a system which appears to me to be unjust; an injustice so independent of personal intentions that each of us profits from it without wishing to do so, and suffers from it without knowing the cause of the suffering."

Three Systems of Plunder

"The sincerity of those who advocate protectionism, socialism, and communism is not here questioned. It is to be pointed out, however, that protectionism, socialism, and communism are basically the same plant in three different stages of its growth."

Law is Force
Law is a Negative Concept
The Political Approach
The Law and Charity
The Law and Education
The Law and Morals

A Confusion of Terms

"Socialism, like the ancient idea from which it springs, confuses the distinction between government and society. As a result of this every time we object to a thing being done by government, the socialists conclude that we object to its being done at all."

The Influence of Socialist Writers
The Socialists Wish to Play God
The Socialists Despise Mankind
Legislators Told How to Manage Men
A Temporary Dictatorship
The Error of Socialist Writers

What is Liberty?

"Actually, what is the political struggle that we witness? It is the instinctive struggle of all people toward liberty. And what is this liberty, whose very name makes the heart beat faster and shakes the world? Is it not the union of all liberties––liberty of conscience, of education, of association, of the press, of travel, of labor, of trade? In short, is not liberty the freedom of every person to make full use of his faculties, so long as he does not harm other persons while doing so? Is not liberty the destruction of all despotism––including, of course, legal despotism? Finally, is not liberty the restricting of the law only to its rational sphere of organizing the right of the individual to lawful self-defense; of punishing injustice?"

Philanthropic Tyranny
The Socialists Want Dictatorship
Dictatorial Arrogance
The Indirect Approach to Depotism
Napoleon Wanted Passive Mankind
The Victims of Socialism
The Doctrine of the Democrats
Socialists Fear All Liberties
The Superman Idea
The Socialists Reject Free Choice
The Cause of the French Revolution
The Enormous Power of Government

CONCLUSION

Politics and Economics

Proper Legislative Functions

"It is not true that the legislator has absolute power over our persons and property. The existence of persons and property preceded the existence of the legislator, and his function is only to guarantee their safety.

"It is not true that the function of law is to regulate our consciences, our ideas, our wills, our education, our opinions, our work, our trade, our talents, or our pleasures. The function of law is to protect the free exercise of these rights, and to prevent any person from interfering with the free exercise of these same rights by any other person.

"Since the law necessarily requires the support of force, its lawful domain is only in the areas where the use of force is necessary. This is justice.

"Every individual has the right to use force for lawful self-defense. It is for this reason that the collective force——which is only the organized combination of the individual forces—may lawfully be used for the same purposes; and it cannot be used legitimately for any other purpose.

"Law is solely the organization of the individual right of self-defense which existed before the law was formalized. Law is justice."

Law and Charity Are Not the Same

"The mission of the law is *not* to oppress persons and plunder them of their property, even though the law may be acting in a philanthropic spirit. Its mission is to protect persons and property."

The High Road to Communism

The Basis for Stable Government

"Law is justice. In this proposition a simple and enduring government can be conceived. And I defy anyone to say how even the thought of revolution, of insurrection, of the slightest uprising could arise against a government whose organized force was confined only to suppressing injustice.

"Under such a regime, there would be the most prosperity—and it would be the most equally distributed. As for the sufferings that are inseparable from humanity, no one would even think of accusing the government for them. This is true because, if the force of government were limited to suppressing injustice, then government would be as innocent of these sufferings as it is now innocent in changes in the temperature."

Justice Means Equal Rights

The Path to Dignity and Progress

"Law is justice. And it is under the law of justice—under the reign of right; under the influence of liberty, safety, stability, and responsibility— that every person will attain his real worth and the true dignity of his being. It is only under this law of justice that mankind will achieve—— slowly, no doubt, but certainly——God's design for the orderly and peaceful progress of humanity.

"It seems to me that this is theoretically right, for whatever the question under discussion——whether religious, philosophical, political, or economic; whether it concerns prosperity, morality, equality, right, justice, progress, responsibility, cooperation, property, labor, trade, capital, wages, taxes, population, finance, or government,——at whatever point on the scientific horizon I begin my researches, I invariably reach this one conclusion: the solution to the problems of human relationships is to be found in liberty."

Proof of an Idea
The Desire to Rule Over Others

Let Us Now Try Liberty

"And now that the legislators and do-gooders have so futilely inflicted so many systems upon society, may they finally end where they should have begun: May they reject all systems, and try liberty; for liberty is an acknowledgement of faith in God and His works."

CHAPTER

VIII

SPECIFIC CHARGES
AND EXAMPLES

This study of *The Modern Conservative* would be incomplete without a discussion of some of the specific charges commonly thrown at all "conservatives." The derogatory charge used most frequently is:

CONSERVATIVES ARE "AGAINST"
INSTEAD OF "FOR"
NEGATIVE NOT *POSITIVE*

This charge, as stated, is largely correct but the evil connotation is decidedly in error for three obvious reasons:

1. For or against depends upon the point of view––being "Against" slavery is being "For" freedom and being "Against" inflation is being "For" sound money.
2. The negative statement often is the only possible clear and simple expression. As examples, note the prohibitions in the Bill of Rights (first ten amendments) of the U. S. Constitution and the "Thou Shalt Not's" in The Ten Commandments.
3. When the vocal leadership is proposing a constant barrage of unwise proposals common sense demands that opposition be

largely negative. It is necessary to stop the foolish propositions before it is possible to develop sound positive progress.

True progress can be built only on a responsible foundation and thus the Free-Enterprise "Conservative" is at a serious disadvantage when competing for backing or votes against a demagogue who glibly presents glittering half-truths.

CONSERVATIVES ARE *FOR* BUSINESS AND *AGAINST* LABOR

This often is more specifically stated as being *for* employers and *against* employees and it assumes the Marxian philosophy that being for one automatically means being against the other. Such automatic opposition is another excellent example of seeing only the immediate and neglecting the long-range results.

"Conservatives" are *for* profitable business since that is the only business which *in the long run* can employ many workers at good wages. They are *against* all practices of either labor or management which limit production, raise costs or lower quality since the final result is harmful to all; owner, worker and customer alike.

CONSERVATIVES OWN STOCK IN COMPANIES PRODUCING WAR MATERIEL THEREFORE *CONSERVATIVES ARE WAR-MONGERS*

This is sheer nonsense. It would be fully as logical to say "Millions of people work at war production—therefore workers are war-mongers."

It is true that most "conservatives" advocate a strong military establishment and deplore all forms of unilateral disarmament but this is because they know that preparedness is the best preventive of war and that weakness is a certain invitation to war, or slavery. For historical proof of this read the little book *Disarm* by Lowell Limpus. For a complete up-to-date analysis read *Peace And Freedom*—Through

Cold War Victory published by The American Security Council after collaboration with 128 colleges and universities, and 102 organizations.

CONSERVATIVES PROPOSE HORSE-AND-BUGGY SOLUTIONS TO VITAL JET-AGE PROBLEMS

This is a straight smear except as it has a basis in the fact that "conservatives" do insist that solutions be in accord with fundamental principles since solutions not in such accord are only temporary expedients which inevitably result in still worse problems. The basis for the smear thus is the "liberal's" contempt for eternal principles which they relegate to "horse-and-buggy" status.

"Conservatives", in general, are fully as kindhearted, generous and desirous of improved wellbeing for everyone as are the "liberals" but the "conservatives" understand the dangers in rash social changes and know that gains which have evolved through centuries of gradual improvement can be lost suddenly. It takes only moments to destroy a living plant or animal which may have been carefully nurtured for years. Also a building or a machine can be damaged beyond repair in far less time and with far less understanding than was required for its production. *Our complex society is no less vulnerable.*

Each increase in governmental control forces a corresponding decrease in the responsibility of the individual and thus, like all acts of destruction, increasing socialism tends to be irreversible. That is, each new socialistic measure causes changes which seem to require still more governmental controls and thus less individual responsibility until freedom is completely lost. The process is almost impossible to stop and reverse since each loss of responsibility tends to weaken the desire for freedom with its corresponding responsibility and only a people with great moral strength and a deep understanding of the eternal truths can surge against the tide and demand individual responsibility. Historically, people have developed this degree of moral strength and understanding only after long periods of severe stress and great tribulation. The entire process is well expressed in this life cycle for civilizations:

1. Bondage develops Spiritual Faith.
2. Spiritual Faith develops Courage.
3. Courage leads to Liberty.
4. Liberty produces Abundance.
5. Abundance relieves stress and promotes Complacency.
6. Complacency leads to Apathy.
7. Apathy refuses responsibility and accepts Dependency.
8. Dependency soon becomes Bondage.

The average time from bondage to liberty and back to bondage has been about 200 years for most civilizations but the time in bondage before sufficient spiritual faith develops may run into many generations. Can we stop our present rush from Apathy to Dependency––and eventual slavery?

Our one hope is to devise an educational program which will give people the necessary understanding and assist in developing their moral strength to the degree required for a gradual return to freedom and responsibility. The alternative is generations of slavery so it behooves *everyone* to exert his best efforts toward this goal. We have no real obligation to leave our children great wealth or social status but we should feel a solemn duty to give them a reasonable opportunity to build a truly peaceful and prosperous society. The decline and fall of any civilization can be averted only if the normal complacency is prevented by an intensive striving toward ever higher goals––spiritual as well as material.

ALL CONSERVATIVES BELIEVE IN
THE CONSPIRACY THEORY

This is about as far as possible from the truth since few "conservatives" have even heard of the conspiracy theory and most of those who have, call it preposterous. In fact, since so little is known of the theory it is necessary to give a very brief outline so that "conservatives" may know what it is that they are supposed to believe.

In essence, the conspiracy theory is that there is a controlling group, usually vaguely named as some international bankers, the Illuminati, or a controlling clique in the CFR (Council of Foreign Relations) who have control of both business and politics in the U.S.A., Britain, France, Italy, etc., and also Russia and all Red Nations. This group is striving for absolute world domination and they, supposedly, maintain the Reds as a strong danger to the Free World so that under the stress of the constantly shifting world tensions they can consolidate their control without any major war or revolution. Some deeply religious people not only believe there is such a group but consider it to be under the direct guidance of Satan himself.

The general consensus of knowledgeable "conservatives" is that the whole theory is preposterous and that it is much more likely that each individual force; Russian Communists, Chinese Communists, British Fabian Socialists, U. S. Welfare Statists, etc., is working for its own supremacy. Any of these groups naturally would work with other groups when it advanced their own aims and still fight the others to keep from being dominated. They all would cooperate against true freedom as advocated by the "conservatives" much as the various Chicago gangs would fight each other for local supremacy but all close ranks against the forces of law and order.

The *theory* of over-all conspiracy must not be confused with the *fact* of communist conspiracy as outlined by J. Edgar Hoover in his famous *Masters Of Deceit* and in dozens of other factual documents including many written by the conspirators themselves. This also holds true for the Fabian Socialists as documented in *Keynes At Harvard* and its sequel *The Great Deceit*, both by the highly respected Veritas Foundation. A more recent book (1966), *Fabian Freeway*––High Road to Socialism in the U.S.A. by Rose L. Martin, is the culmination of years of serious research into the hidden machinations which now have us travelling at high speed down that deadly freeway. It exposes and analyses the hidden interlocks and includes extensive Index, Bibliography and six Appendices.

Probably the reason the *theory* of the conspiracy is believed at all is that, using jigsaw puzzle terms, if you build toward that picture the pieces all fit together with no blank spaces of unanswered questions—except the big one of why any human being would want to wreck our whole civilization for just a little temporary power. (The Satan involvement could answer that also).

THE CONSERVATIVE OPPOSES
THE WELFARE STATE
THE WELFARE STATE HELPS PEOPLE
THEREFORE
THE CONSERVATIVE OPPOSES
SOCIAL PROGRESS

This general idea underlies the mass appeal of the "liberals" and the consequent difficulty in electing "conservatives." The first statement is true, the second partly true and the third completely false.

The welfare state obviously helps some people, at least temporarily, but its hidden and long-range effects are harmful both economically and morally to the general public and even to most of the recipients.

The Constitution of the U.S. was framed in accordance with natural law—the eternal truths. The Founding Fathers were thoroughly familiar with the history of previous civilizations and they had basic understanding of what caused each to flourish and fall. They did not know the details of atomic physics but they knew full well that there were fixed laws which governed the universe and that these laws covered economic and moral as well as strictly physical activities.

Natural laws (economic and moral as well as physical) act without regard to personal status or motives and often the results are contrary to expectations. A simple example is the "population explosion" which results when modern sanitation and improved diet are introduced suddenly to a backward people who have a stable population with about one baby out of five reaching adulthood and having children. When the "boon" of science allows three or four of the five babies to reach adulthood it is only some twenty years until there will be three to four times as many young adults and shortly thereafter three to four times again as many babies, etc. etc.

A less obvious, but no less dangerous, change is the shift in population growth within a specific group of people. Natural law often is referred to as insuring "the survival of the fittest" since in nature there is a definite tendency for the wiser and stronger specimens to out-reproduce those who are less versatile.

Any man-made law or practice which works against natural trends must be given careful scrutiny. As an example, note the various humanitarian laws and practices which in the last generation have so aided the lowest (economic and moral) segments of our society that now they greatly out-reproduce the top quality elements. The result is just beginning to attract general attention but if continued for long it is certain to drastically reduce our moral standards as well as our economic well-being. The rapidly increasing crime rate, especially of teenagers, gives a slight preview of the future.

These items go back to an understanding of basic morality so we shall digress a moment to consider this aspect in more detail.

THE MORAL ISSUE

If, as seems obvious, morality consists in practices which are in full accord with natural law, i.e., with the laws of the God of all creation which tend toward the improvement and perfection of everything which lives, then practices which clearly negate such principles require a most critical consideration.

The modern "conservative" who has sufficient depth of understanding to foresee the inherent long-range evil results has serious doubts as to the morality of many "liberal" demands.

Is it moral to make it not only possible, but practical and even quite profitable, for the lowest elements in any society to reproduce at double or triple the rate of the highest elements and thus in a few generations swamp that society into mediocrity?

Is it moral to give a broad increase in voting rights to millions of ignorant people of low culture and thus throw many communities and possibly even some entire states under their control (or rather under the control of the demagogues who usually exploit such people)?

Is it moral to vastly improve the hygiene of backward nations without equivalent improvement in economic knowledge and in morality so that they can have at least some chance to cope with the resulting population explosion?

Is it moral to give labor bosses political and economic power to force up wages and curtail production with consequent unemployment and reduced national prosperity?

CONSERVATIVES OBJECT TO ACADEMIC FREEDOM

This is an ideal example of semantic reversal since "conservatism" is based on deep understanding and thus requires *maximum* academic freedom. Many "liberal" professors actually believe the fallacies and half-truths they preach but the really knowledgeable socialists simply con the public in their drive for power. Both go to unbelievable lengths to discredit opposing views, and the books listed on page 233 are filled with tragic examples.

The "liberal" professor has a very real stake in socialism where the professor-politician combination is king—with consumers and businessmen alike simply serfs who perform as directed. This is very different from free enterprise where the consumer is boss—with professors, politicians and businessmen simply servants whose pay is determined largely by the service rendered.

Under true academic freedom each idea or policy may be subjected to searching scrutiny to insure that long-range and obscure eventualities will be brought to light and become known and understood equally with the immediate and obvious results. This is a main objective of true "conservatives" but it is poison to all socialists since socialism is based on the half-truths of neglecting all but the immediate and obvious. Allowing a communist to speak on campus is actual negation of academic freedom since it permits the skillful presentation of plausible fallacies without any possibility of adequate exposure.

CONSERVATIVES ARE AGAINST
CIVIL RIGHTS

This is another typical semantic twist. Most "Conservatives" are solidly *for* full constitutional equality of opportunity for all *responsible* citizens without regard to race, color or religion. They are *against* riots, sit-ins, lie-ins, mass demonstrations and all other acts which arouse hate, fear and distrust between peoples.

"Conservatives" desire to build responsibility and integrity in everyone so that increasing freedom and prosperity may be enjoyed by all. The emotional rush to obtain "rights" before developing the necessary corresponding responsibility is one of the great catastrophes of this age. It is a result of concentrating on an immediate objective with no regard for ultimate results.

The "Civil Rights" demonstrations for voting privileges also follow from the unconstitutional and unwise expansion of government into social action. In 1850 Bastiat outlined the devastating results which must follow such actions (as noted briefly in the previous chapter). If Government was restricted as advocated by Bastiat, and by most "conservatives," the ignorant would have no desire to vote as it would be obvious even to them that it was to their advantage to have only the wisest people in control. With government actively engaged in the social transfer of wealth it at least seems necessary for each group to maximize its voting power to insure getting its share of the plunder.

Since all but a few are ignorant of even basic economic principles it is obvious that the masses will vote themselves an excessive share of production and thus radically curtail profits. Reducing profits reduces the incentive to save thus reducing the capital available for tools which are essential to increased production. The result is similar to eating the seed corn and then wailing because there is such a small crop the next year.

The difference between "conservative" and "liberal" is very evident in the different emphasis placed on "right-to-work" and "right-to-vote." The "liberal" has no compunction about restricting the right to work as that is considered more of a property right and thus of a lower order than the human right of voting.

The "conservative" looks past the emotional issues to the basic values. If a person has a right to live he must have the right to sustain his life (his work) and the right to the results of his work––his property. Thus the rights of life, work and property are indivisible for *free* men and are the base on which all other rights are founded. Voting is not even an inherent right. It is a privilege granted by democratic societies to those citizens deemed qualified, and when voting qualifications are too low it is almost certain that scheming politicians will mislead the ignorant masses and use them in their drive for power.

CONSERVATIVES REJECT INTEGRATION

"Conservatives" believe in free, not forced association since they know that free association develops respect and goodwill while forced association breeds fear and hate. When the issue is clearly drawn and all arguments well presented, most Americans can see past the immediate and obvious even when respected leaders fog the issue with charges of bigotry.

An excellent example is the 1964 vote in California on Proposition 14––an initiative act to repeal an outrageous forced-housing law and allow property owners to rent or sell to whomsoever they wished. The forced housing law gave a state board complete power to decide if any prospective tenant or purchaser was refused because of race, religion, etc., and even authorized up to a $500 payment to anyone who turned in such a case.

Proposition 14 passed by a two to one vote and an analysis of this vote with others on the same ballot indicates that each side had nearly equal strong votes "on principle" and minor votes "on hate" with the deciding block of voters not understanding the deep principles involved but just using common sense. These five groups were:

1. Some two million "conservatives" who voted for free association strictly on principle.

2. A small fraction of a million racists and bigots who voted (against integration) strictly on hate. These were counterbalanced by group

3. Another couple of million, led by many of the ministers who were so opposed to the hate and bigotry of those in group #2 that they gave no consideration to the profoundly moral arguments of those in the first group. Neither did they realize that they themselves were directly aligned with the far more dangerous group

4. Consisting of a few tens of thousands of socialists and communists and their fellow travelers. The socialists openly considered the state controlled housing law as a keystone in their plans to socialize the country. Many ex-FBI agents reported that the absolute top priority for California communists was the defeat of Proposition 14 and this was confirmed by the extensive coverage given this topic in all communist publications. The communists fully understood that the forced housing law would be a continual source of conflict——a constant trouble breeder. The decisive vote was cast by group

5. Another couple of million who did not fully understand the basic freedom principles involved but who had lived in apartments (or had friends in apartments) and from first-hand experience knew full well that the apartment manager must discriminate or the apartment soon becomes unlivable. This does not mean unreasoning bias against any race or religion but just plain honest discrimination to insure that any new tenants will be reasonably acceptable to their neighbors.

CHAPTER

IX

FREEDOM—RESPONSIBILITY— INTEGRITY & PEACE

THE BELEAGUERED CITY

The vignette of the invaded city is an excellent example of long-range reversal. According to the story, this city in Western Europe was at the fringe of the invasion by Eastern Barbarians. As the invaders approached, the surrounding farmers and villagers flocked into the city with all possible food and other goods and the local merchants stocked up to the limit with little regard for cost.

Naturally the people complained bitterly against the high prices so the religious and civil leaders in solemn conference classed all such price increases as treason in such perilous times and forced a price reduction on pain of death to any profiteer. The people promptly purchased their allotted rations and the stores were empty. Soon the people again were without food and demanded food at any price. The leaders then cancelled the price control laws and ordered the merchants to obtain food but the daredevil blockade runners had left and there was no way to obtain more food so the barbarians captured the weakened city.

The healthiest men, women and older children were herded off as slaves and the rest were tortured and killed for the sport of the invaders. Most of us feel great compassion for even such stupid people but a cynic might consider that the invaders should have honored the leaders for passing the law which stopped all inflow of food and thus insured the fall of the city.

The tale of the sacked city is not a direct parable for our present situation but indirectly, and with much longer time between cause and effect, there are far too many similarities.

The United States of America is the one final citadel which blocks complete world domination by the Eastern Barbarians––atheistic, savage communism. People from subjugated countries daily give up all material possessions and even risk their lives to escape from communism. Others not yet captured try desperately to reach the U.S.A.

Almost a century ago we passed a few laws which eroded States Rights and gave a small start to the shift toward the strong central government required by collectivism. Fifty years later the seemingly innocuous Income Tax Amendment laid the foundation for Welfare State Collectivism.

The Great Depression (1929-39) opened the doors of government to all sorts of socialistic quacks, and subservient congresses have passed a continual stream of such legislation that Norman Thomas, perennial candidate of the Socialist Party, claims that over 85% of their basic program is now law.

The Great Society is the most recent name for our rush into the collectivist, socialistic Welfare State. The purported features of all such programs are to "improve the general welfare," especially of those who have much less than average income, wealth and ability. The actual features, however, run in three main directions:

1. Shift responsibility from the individual to the group, and from the small group to the larger group.
2. Shift economic power from those who have proven their ability to create wealth (the haves) to those who lack that ability (the have nots).
3. Shift political power from those who understand long-range reversals and the necessity for developing individual responsibility and personal integrity to those who have no such depth of understanding.

These seem to be quite distinct but each aids and supplements the others. The shift in responsibility assists, and also follows from, the shift in economic power and the shift in political power assists, and follows from, the shift in both economic power and responsibility.

The vital factor, which is seldom mentioned, is that individual freedom-to-choose and its corollary, personal responsibility for the results of such choice, are the essential building blocks of personal integrity. *Without freedom to choose there can be no personal responsibility and without a deep sense of personal responsibility there is little hope for much personal integrity.*

Our tremendously productive economy is based on the specialized division of highly tooled labor and this in turn requires a high general degree of personal integrity. This is the deadly time-bomb which is being loaded with greater explosive power by every added piece of "helpful" legislation which always reduces individual responsibility and thus, eventually, integrity. The delay period approaches a generation for this type of action so the rapid rise in juvenile delinquency and crime in general might well be attributed to the "welfare" legislation of the 1930's and 40's. The results of the rapidly increasing "social" legislation of the 50's and 60's may not reach full effect for another decade or so but the current student demonstrations and scattered major riots give some warning of what may follow.

A recent newspaper article, headlined "Amazing Paradox" told how surprised and shocked a prominent psychologist was that people were not responding properly to all of the tremendous help now offered. He could not understand why people were not avidly striving to make full use of the proliferation of wonderful educational and business opportunities for advancement; why people seem less interested in striving and more interested in getting something for nothing and why delinquency and crime were increasing rapidly in spite of all the various forms of aid.

It would seem that his thoughts do not go much deeper than the "immediate and the obvious" or he would understand that continued aid coupled with the inherent shift to others of responsibility is bound to reduce both the desire and the ability of the individual to accept responsibility and that this withering of responsibility also means a similar withering of personal integrity. Thus the increased crime and delinquency is no paradox but is an inherent result which inevitably must follow coddling; and with the great increase in all forms of aid (coddling) we can logically expect that the crime and delinquency rate will continue to increase rapidly.

The truly amazing paradox is the tremendous number of supposedly highly intelligent clergy and educators who preach and teach the socialist philosophy of forcibly taking from the haves (the highly productive) to give to the have-nots (the non-productive) and seemingly haven't the slightest notion that they are working diligently to undermine incentive and kill individual responsibility and personal integrity.

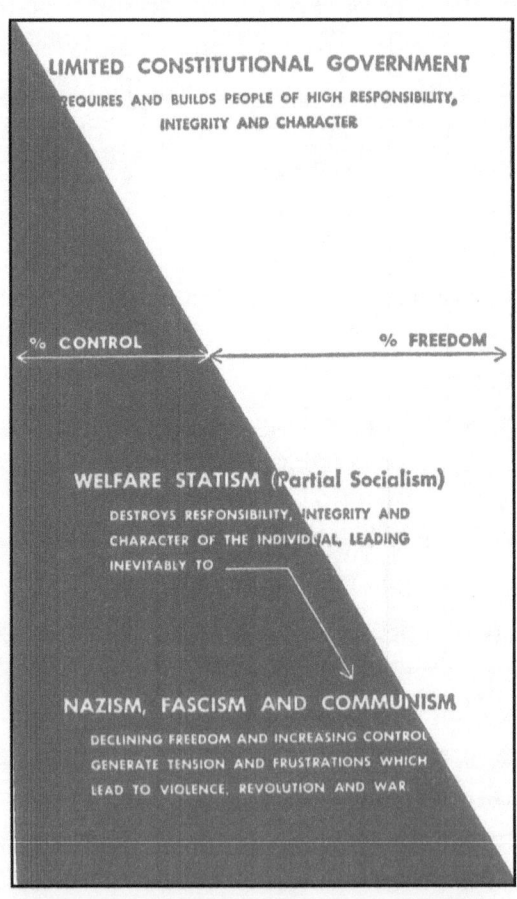

There is much discussion about LEFT and RIGHT today. The widely held belief that Nazism and Fascism are the ultimate Far Right and thus the opposite of communism, the ultimate Far Left, is an outstanding communist fallacy. Actually, both Nazism and Fascism are forms of national socialism and thus are almost identical to communism, which is international socialism. Any imagined ideal middle position between communism and fascism is non-existent.

A more realistic classification can be made along a scale of Individual Freedom, with 100% freedom at the top and zero freedom, 100% state control, at the bottom. On such a scale, communism, Nazism and fascism would be located near the bottom along with other absolute dictatorships. On up the scale would come the various degrees of welfare statism (partial socialism) followed by a jump to severely limited constitutional government. The absence of any restrictive government would be at the very top.

LIBERTY--RESPONSIBILITY--INTEGRITY

The above classification illustrates many important truths. One is that there seems to be an all-pervading force, something like gravity, which inclines all governments to increase their power at the expense of individual freedom. This is well stated in the adage, "eternal vigilance is the price of liberty." By the same token, for every step up the ladder of freedom, the individuals in any society must accept a corresponding increase in personal responsibility. If the added freedom is taken without responsibility, it becomes license. Social existence then becomes intolerable and the government must restrict the freedom of those who will not act responsibly. From this it is obvious that freedom can be increased only as the individuals in a society develop their personal integrity and their willingness to accept responsibility.

It is well understood by collectivists that when people lose personal integrity and become unwilling and unable to accept responsibility, they not only must be controlled but will demand to have controls. This is one reason why the communists and all such power seekers first undermine religion, patriotism and family, promote all forms of juvenile and adult delinquency and advocate broad welfare programs. This pattern shows clearly in the decline of every recorded civilization.

It is obvious that individual freedom to choose and personal responsibility are directly related since responsibility cannot properly be placed where there is no freedom to choose. It is just as true, although not so obvious, that personal integrity is directly related to acceptance of responsibility. An individual's constant acceptance of responsibility gradually builds integrity while the constant avoidance of it steadily weakens integrity. Thus, a slight undermining of the foundations of morality, aided by broad social welfare activity, slowly weakens general personal integrity. This further undermines morality and increases the demand for more welfare and controls. The process naturally accelerates into a precipitous slide to complete collectivism. It can be stopped only if enough citizens become aware of what is happening and take a firm stand for a return to basic morality and strict constitutional government.

To regain all lost liberties will take many years of intensive search for knowledge and understanding. Even the freedom of limited constitutional government cannot be restored until the general morality improves and people again realize the necessity for personal integrity and the full acceptance of individual responsibility. The strangest part of this tragedy is that so many of our highly rated intellectuals, especially educators and clergy who should be the foremost advocates of liberty and morality, are now the most effective exponents of socialism. This is causing serious cleavage in many congregations.

LIBERTY—PEACE

Another vital, but little understood, relationship is the direct connection between Liberty and Peace. It is inherently impossible for a government to be aggressive if it is restricted to the protection of individual liberty, and it is just as impossible for a socialistic government with its necessary controls over everyone to keep from generating the frustrations and tensions which lead to revolution and war.

✧ (End of Quote)

Every individual interested in peace (and everyone should be so interested for both humane and economic reasons) should take careful note of the above fact. War with its limitless injury and death approaches the ultimate in inhumanity and its almost total dislocation and massive destruction is entirely uneconomic. Since both history and simple logic show that increasing socialism sharply increases the probability of war (note the starters of all recent major and minor conflicts) one would expect every thinking person to be fighting socialism but actually almost the reverse is true.

It is a sad commentary on our educational system that even the communist socialists can use "Peace" as the most effective bait for intellectuals. This is a horrible example of the "big lie" technique and every student should be trained to spot such fallacies. It cannot be overemphasized that IT IS IMPOSSIBLE FOR A GOVERNMENT TO BE AGGRESSIVE IF IT IS RESTRICTED TO THE PROTECTION OF INDIVIDUAL LIBERTY.

The lack of understanding of the fallacies of socialism which places such a large percentage of both educators and clergy in the "liberal" category, actively teaching and preaching socialism, may be due to the reduced status of these professions. Two centuries ago when all schools were church affiliated and the leading preachers were driving home in their sermons the basic truths which later were distilled into our Declaration of Independence and Constitution only top students dared aspire to such heights. Today the situation has largely changed. Now most brilliant students aspire to be scientists, engineers, doctors, lawyers, etc., and, with far too few outstanding exceptions, many of those becoming preachers and teachers are second and third raters who are afraid to tackle the hard jobs and thus gravitate toward the relatively easy subjects and the greater security offered.

This trend has deadly implications since the teachers and preachers mold the ideas and ideals of each generation and if they are shallow thinkers with little understanding of fundamental truths and of the absolute necessity for individual freedom, responsibility, and integrity it would appear that there is little chance for the moral revival which must precede a resurgence of freedom.

Some of these leaders are so enamored of their exalted position that they easily convince themselves that they have the wisdom and deep understanding which should be associated therewith and thus they refuse to even consider any constructive ideas. Their minds are made up and must not be confused with facts. Most of them, however, require only two simple items to effect a distinct "about face." a) The opportunity to learn the fundamental "why" of conservatism—the basic understanding of economic and moral laws and the necessity for individual freedom, and b) the assurance that respected citizens will give full and complete support to their efforts at communicating this knowledge and understanding to others since the collectivists and their many dupes will attack and smear all such efforts.

The "information explosion" adds to the problem since knowledge is increasing at such a rate that even top intellectuals can barely keep abreast of all developments in even narrowly specialized fields and thus they feel obliged to stick to their own specialty and steer clear of any controversy with other professions. The future for freedom would appear dark indeed except for *you* and a very few million others who, like you, do have some depth of understanding of these fundamental truths and *have the courage and conviction to do something about it.*